View of the City of Ely in the County of Cambridge. Engraved for *The Modern Universal British Traveller* (1779).

THE RIVER GREAT OUSE

AND THE RIVER CAM

A Pictorial History
from Brackley to King's Lynn

Houghton Mill, *c.*1914.

THE RIVER GREAT OUSE

AND THE RIVER CAM

A Pictorial History
from Brackley to King's Lynn

Josephine Jeremiah

Phillimore

2006

Published by
PHILLIMORE & CO. LTD
Shopwyke Manor Barn, Chichester, West Sussex, England
www.phillimore.co.uk

ISBN   1-86077-417-2
ISBN 13   978-1-86077-417-1

Printed and bound in Great Britain by
CAMBRIDGE PRINTING

List of Illustrations

Frontispiece: Houghton Mill, *c.*1914

v

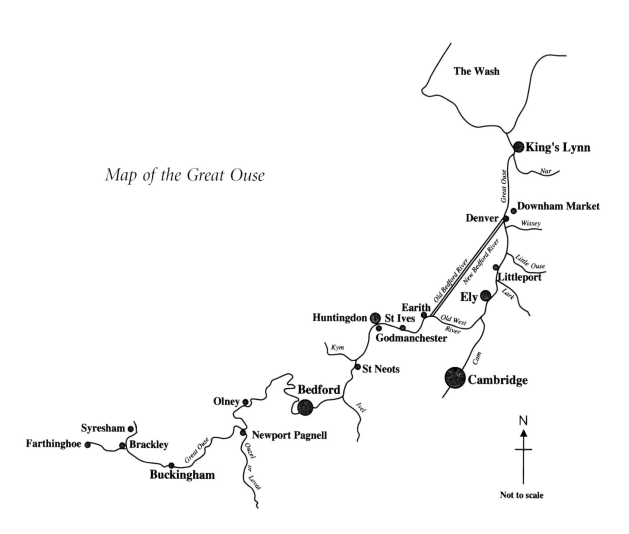

Map of the Great Ouse

An Historical Journey

The River Great Ouse rises in Northamptonshire. From its source near Brackley, the river runs south-east to Buckingham and then it flows in a generally north-easterly direction through Bedford, St Neots, Huntingdon, St Ives, Earith, Ely and Littleport to Denver Sluice, after which it heads north to King's Lynn and the Wash. At Pope's Corner it is joined by the River Cam, while the Rivers Lark, Little Ouse, Wissey and Nar are other main tributaries. The course of the main river below Earith is very different from what it was in early medieval times when its outfall to the Wash was at Wisbech. Silting up of the Wisbech estuary caused the river to change course and head for the sea near King's Lynn. More change came with the drainage of the Fens, in the mid-17th century.

Some believe that the Great Ouse originates to the west of Brackley. Others think it emerges either to the north-west or north-east of the town. Nicholson's *Ordnance Survey Guide to the Broads & Fens* (1986) noted the source as being two miles west of Silverstone and Ordnance Survey maps label the River Great Ouse to the north-east of Brackley. However, C.F. Farrar, the author of *Ouse's Silent Tide* (1921), thought that the beginning of the river was north-west of Brackley, near Farthinghoe. It was here that he tracked the source of a tiny brook, which he believed to be the infant Great Ouse, and found it 'gushing up in gouts of water'.

Brackley is the first town on the bank of the Great Ouse and was settled in two different areas. The earliest part of Brackley, around St Peter's parish church, dates from Roman times, while a second community grew up close to the early medieval castle near the river. A description of the town is given by the 16th-century writer John Leland:

> I enteryd into *Brakeley* by a little Stone Bridge in a Botom, of one Arche, undar the whiche *Use* Rivert rennithe, there being a letle Streame. From this Bridge the great Streate of the Towne goith up apon a pratie Hille: at the Pitch whereof there turnithe a nothar Streat by Este to Seint *Peter's*, the Heade Churche of the Towne … There was a fayre Castle in the Southe-West End of the Towne, on the left Hand or Ripe of the Riveret. The Site and Hille where it stode is yet evidently sene, and berithe the Name of the *Castle Hill*; but there is not sene any Peace of a Waull stondinge.

The New and Complete English Traveller (1794) observed, 'This town is greatly decayed from what it was in former times, when it was particularly celebrated for its great trade in wool.' In the late 18th century, there were, however, still some remains of its ancient grandeur in its two parish churches and free grammar school. The latter was founded in the 15th century and maintained by the president and fellows of Magdalen College, Oxford. The school still exists today as Magdalen College School. *Pigot & Co.'s Commercial Directory* of 1830 was not so complimentary about the town recording that, apart from the two churches of St Peter and St James, 'The town possesses but little to recommend it to the observation of the tourist: its buildings have no pretension to uniformity or architectural taste'. St Peter's Church, dating from Norman times, still stands, but the church of St James is no more.

C.F. Farrar, the author of *Ouse's Silent Tide*, his son C.B. and their companion, Colonel Young, set off on a voyage by canoe down the Great Ouse at the end of May in 1920. After carting their canoes from Brackley railway station, they started at Evenley, but all was not plain sailing. During the first day's travel, there were 'four mill porterages, two impassable bridges, and *fifteen* obstacle porterages'. Eventually, they reached Buckingham's *White Horse Hotel*, 'exhausted by 12 hours of battle'. Next day, the author was told by an ancient 'Bookinghamite' that no boat had ever come before from Brackley and that there was not a single boat to be found in 'Bookingham'.

The Universal British Directory of Trade, Commerce and Manufacture (1791) described **Buckingham** as 'situated in a valley, on a dry gravelly soil, surrounded on all sides, except the North, by the Ouze, over which are three stone bridges'. It noted that the spire of the church, reckoned one of the tallest in England, was blown down in 1698, by a tempest, and never rebuilt. After the tower of this church fell, on 26 March 1776, a new church was erected on the hill where Buckingham's castle formerly stood.

Forty years later, Samuel Lewis wrote about Buckingham in *A Topographical Dictionary of England* (1831) and noted: 'it consists principally of one long street; the houses in general are built of brick, and the town is paved, lighted with oil, and plentifully supplied with water. The trade chiefly consists in sorting wool, tanning leather and the making of lace … A branch of the Grand Junction canal, extending to the town, affords the means of supplying it with coal, and considerably facilitates trade.'

A focal point at Buckingham is the Old Gaol, which is now the museum and tourist centre. Another interesting feature of the town is its riverside walk, along which there is a variety of wildlife. The river is the habitat of dragonflies, swans, moorhens and mallards, while the quick blue flash of a kingfisher is sometimes seen. The Great Ouse winds around Fisher's Field then passes under Castle Bridge and Lords Bridge before making its way to London Road Bridge, which was opened in 1805. The construction of the latter was paid for by the Marquis of Buckingham, the east side of the bridge displaying the coat of arms of the Temple-Grenville family of Stowe, the great country house, now a public school, which is just three miles from the town.

In past times, there were corn mills, driven by water power, in the town. These included the Castle Mill, rebuilt in 1897 and destroyed by fire in 1964, which once stood by Castle Bridge. There was also the Old Town Mill, downstream of Lords Bridge, which dates from 1782 and is now part of Buckingham University, and Bourton Mill, on the edge of Bourton Park, at present housing a health club.

After Bourton Mill, on their second day of voyaging C.F. Farrar and his fellow canoeists still had three more mills to pass before reaching Stony Stratford for the night. These were Maidsmorton, Thornborough and Thornton. They found Maidsmorton 'a lonely, desolate, disused mill', but at Thornborough Mill the author met the miller who had a 'perfectly constructed eel trap', which gave him enough fish to feed his household. Not only eels were caught in it, but carp and salmon trout, too. At last, after a day's voyage of 17 miles, the canoeists came in sight of the long causeway and bridge of Stony Stratford, carrying the Roman road of Watling Street across the great expanse of water meadows, which would be flooded in winter.

Stony Stratford, in Buckinghamshire, is built along this old Roman road. *The Universal British Directory* of 1791 noted Stony Stratford as being 'on the great Chester and Liverpool road' and described it as 'a mile in length including Old Stratford, which is in Northamptonshire, being divided only by a stone-bridge across the river Ouse, which separates the counties of Northamptonshire and Bucks'. At this time, there was no manufacturing carried on in the town, other than lace making among the female inhabitants, and the town depended on the road and the market for its main support. On Fridays, a great deal of butchers' meat was sold in the market, while great quantities of corn were bought and sold on market days when the farmers and corn factors brought samples to several public houses where the chief business of the corn trade took place.

1 Great Ouse, Stony Stratford, *c*.1909. The message on the back of this old postcard reads, 'You can see it is very flat round here but rather pretty. We went otter hunting in this river this morning but we didn't have much sport.'

The *Cock* and the *Bull*, two inns near the middle of the town, were described in *The Universal British Directory* as 'both very neat and roomy buildings', which were 'furnished with every necessary accommodation'. The excise office was at the *Bull*, while the post office was at the *Cock*. The Coventry, Liverpool, Chester and Birmingham coaches passed through Stony Stratford every day. Wagons also passed in great numbers with frequently twelve in a week from Manchester alone.

C.F. Farrar's canoeing party stayed in one of the town's inns overnight having to be content with 'the omni-present ham and eggs', which appears to have been the usual fare for travellers. On the third day, their river journey was to be from Stony Stratford to Olney. Having left Stony Stratford, the author of *Ouse's Silent Tide* mentioned passing under the 'great viaduct' carrying the Grand Junction Canal over the Great Ouse. A 'bargee' on this aqueduct overhead hailed the canoeists with the comment that he hadn't seen any boat go under the aqueduct for 20 years.

By the second half of the 19th century **Wolverton**, a settlement on the Great Ouse to the north-east of Stony Stratford, had grown considerably. This was due to the erection of large workshops, foundries and factories where locomotive engines and carriages were repaired. These works employed a great number of hands. The central locomotive depot for the London and North Western Railway was here and the line was carried across the Great Ouse by a viaduct with a length of 660ft. In the mid-1860s, locomotive building and maintenance work was stopped at Wolverton and transferred to Crewe, while carriage works at Birmingham were vacated and this business was transferred to Wolverton.

Twelve and a half miles was the distance, which the canoeists travelled by water between Stony Stratford and Newport Pagnell. The same journey by road would have been six miles. During the trip, one of the canoes struck a snag, which made a hole the size of a half crown. This had to be patched with a piece of sticking plaster and the waterlogged canoe was towed behind the other, which now held all three voyagers. Luckily, a bicycle-tyre mending kit was procured at Newport Pagnell and, with this and some hot pitch, the hole was patched again.

At the time of Domesday Book, **Newport Pagnell** was known as just Newport and was held by William, son of Ansculf de Picquigny. The second part of its name is derived from the Pagnells, who were lords of the manor some years after the Norman Conquest. The town is situated at the confluence of the Great Ouse and the River Lovat or Ouzel, the latter being crossed by a cast-iron bridge at the entrance to the town by the London road, while a stone bridge crosses the Great Ouse on the road from Northampton. Water transport brought coal to Newport Pagnell in the early 19th century, but this fuel was brought by canal rather than river. In 1815, a new cut was started from Great Linford on the Grand Junction Canal. The Newport Pagnell Canal, with six locks, was opened in 1817 with wharfage in the town known as Shipley Wharf after the coal mines in Shipley, Derbyshire whence the coal, brought by narrowboats, came. This canal closed in 1864 and a railway was built over part of the canal bed.

Newport Pagnell was once a centre for the lace industry. In the 17th century, linen thread and patterns were supplied to workers in their homes and lacemen would take the finished lace to London where a great amount was worn by both sexes in fashionable society. Lace making at Newport Pagnell continued through the 18th century and into the 19th century. In *Newport Pagnell: A Pictorial History* (1995), Dennis Mynard and Julian Hunt noted that, by 1851, there were still 316 lacemakers in the town at a time when the lace trade was suffering from the competition of Nottingham lace, which was made by machines.

From Newport Pagnell, the Great Ouse loops around to the stone-built 18th-century Sherington Bridge. C.F. Farrar, in *Ouse's Silent Tide*, recorded that after Sherington Bridge there began 'a stately stretch of river, broader and far more beautiful than anything to be seen from Brackley to Lynn', which flowed 'in perfect solitude, unspoilt by boats or river parties, the wild life of its banks unmarred as if it were a primeval river'. A one-arched bridge crosses the river at **Tyringham**. This bridge, like Tyringham Hall and its gateway on the right bank, was designed by John Soane in the late 18th century though the house was altered in the early 1900s. Gayhurst House, an Elizabethan mansion, is on the opposite side of the river from Tyringham. Sir Everard Digby, an early owner, was one of the conspirators connected with the Gunpowder Plot in the reign of James I. In January 1606, he was sentenced to death for his part in the conspiracy and, after being hung, drawn and quartered, the remains of his body were exhibited on Tower Hill in London.

After **Gayhurst**, the river flows north-east between **Emberton**, on the right bank, and **Weston Underwood**, on the left, both settlements lying back from the river. It was to Weston Underwood that the 18th-century poet, William Cowper, moved in 1786, with his long-time companion Mrs Unwin. They took up residence at Weston Lodge after 19 years in Olney, where the poet had rented the house called Orchard Side.

In **Olney**, William Cowper wrote many of his celebrated works including *The Task* in which there is reference to the river:

> Here Ouse, slowly winding through a level plain
> Of spacious meads, with cattle sprinkled o'er,
> Conducts the eye along his sinuous course
> Delighted. There, fast rooted in their bank,
> Stand, never overlooked, our favourite elms,
> That screen the herdsman's solitary hut;
> While far beyond, and overthwart the stream,
> That, as with molten glass, inlays the vale,
> The sloping land recedes into the clouds;
> Displaying on its varied side the grace
> Of hedgerow beauties numberless, square tower,
> Tall spire, from which the sound of cheerful bells
> Just undulates upon the listening ear;
> Groves, heaths, and smoking villages remote.

Noted for the Cowper and Newton Museum, which is situated in William Cowper's former residence, alongside the Market Place, the town is also renowned for its Pancake Race. The latter is a tradition, which dates back to a Shrove Tuesday in the 15th century, when a townswoman, who is said to have been making pancakes, ran outside with her frying pan on hearing the bell ring for church service. Olney's Pancake Race still takes place on Shrove Tuesday and the course is from the Market Place to the parish church of St Peter and St Paul. One of the rules of the race is that a pancake has to be tossed, once at the beginning and once during the race.

In past times, lace manufacture was carried on at Olney, to a considerable extent. The hours worked by the lacemakers were long and hard, but they had a day off work on St Andrew's Day, known locally as Tanders Day, when they took part in celebrations held in the town. On that day much metheglin, a mead-like beverage, was consumed. In the *Heart and Soul of Olney* (2004), Lewis Kitchener devoted a chapter to Olney Lace, from its beginnings when, centuries ago, lacemakers from the continent settled in the area, to one of the last of the lace dealers in the town, Harry Armstrong, who worked in the trade in the early 20th century and who died in 1943.

Leaving Olney, the Great Ouse flows under the 19th-century Olney Bridge on the south side of the town. C.F. Farrar, in *Ouse's Silent Tide*, remarked, 'Ouse winds away as sinuously from Olney as it approached it, and it is a long time before we lose Olney Church from view.' The canoeists had reached Olney on the evening of the third day of their river trip. On the fourth day, their route took them past the picturesque mill of **Lavendon**, or 'Larndon' as it was known locally, before reaching the 'gaunt, burnt-out ruin' of Turvey Mill. Here they saw the statue of Jonah on the Mill Pool with a big fish at his feet. It was a Whit Monday and there was a crowd of children paddling around Jonah. The canoeists sheltered from the sun and wind under the bridge for their lunch. However, the author felt that the urchins sitting on the parapet above were likely to make mischief by spitting at them. On threatening them with the name of the great lady of the parish, ten pairs of boot soles vanished and all was peace again.

After paddling four miles from **Turvey**, along fine broad reaches, the canoeists reached **Harrold**, the first village, in the author's opinion, which really ventured to settle directly on the banks of the river. The ancient bridge here links Harrold, on the north bank of the river, with Carlton on the south bank. A few miles downstream, another bridge crosses the Great Ouse at **Felmersham** and there is a 13th-century ironstone church dedicated to St Mary. It was at Felmersham that the canoeists had a slight shock to their nerves, which had been lulled by four days voyaging along lonely river reaches. Here, they first encountered others boating on the river as a few ancient painted boats and one punt were let out for hire. A gramophone, an undesirable feature of river life, had also been provided, on that Whit Monday, by the boat hirer. All along the stretch of the river to **Sharnbrook**, there were families having picnics and anglers and bathers enjoying themselves. The canoeists, themselves, had the luxury of tea at the *Falcon* at **Bletsoe**, which was their destination on the fourth day of travelling.

At Felmersham, the Great Ouse starts a series of meanders. Being on the right bank, this village is almost encircled by the first of these loops of the river, while Sharnbrook and Bletsoe are situated on the outer side of the meander, on the left bank. At the end of this first loop, the Great Ouse flows under Radwell Bridge and then makes a course in the shape of an 'S' to Stafford Bridge, passing **Milton Ernest**. On his fifth day of travelling down the Great Ouse, C.F. Farrar noted that **Pavenham**, the next settlement downstream, still retained one of the few surviving ancient industries of the river, namely the making of osier baskets and rush matting.

Past **Stevington** on the right bank, the Great Ouse is crossed by the five-arched bridge at **Oakley**, a village on the left bank. It was here that the river rose 16 feet above its normal level on 31 October and 1 November 1823, drowning many sheep and cattle and damaging corn in the barns. The road across the bridge at Oakley leads to **Bromham**, which has a medieval bridge over the river. Once known as Biddenham Bridge, as it links the settlement of **Biddenham** with Bromham, this long stone bridge, with its recesses for pedestrians, is now called Bromham Bridge. Before Bedford is reached, the Great Ouse passes the riverside church of All Saints at **Kempston** and the site of Kempston Mill. The latter is the limit of navigation for small craft and there is a place to wind by the railway bridge, which is west of Town Bridge, for cruisers and narrowboats coming upriver.

Bedford was the final destination for C.F. Farrar and his fellow canoeists on their five-day voyage down the Great Ouse at Whitsun in 1920. Using one-inch, and in some cases, in Bedfordshire, six-inch maps, C.F. Farrar and his canoeing companion, Colonel Young, calculated the distances they had boated during their time on the river. Allowing for the 'intricate sinuosities of the river' and bearing in mind other irregularities such as avoiding reeds, rushes, snags and fallen trees, they reckoned that the distance from Farthinghoe to Bedford was a total of 102½ miles and that from Brackley to Bedford was 95½ miles.

The town of Bedford was described in *A New Display of the Beauties of England* (1773):

> BEDFORD is forty-eight miles from London and is the county-town, being a clean, well-built, and populous place. The town, as well as the county, is divided into two parts by the River Ouse, which crosses it in the direction of east and west: the north and south parts of the town are joined by a stone bridge, which has two gates … There are five churches here, three on the north, and two on the south side of the river. The chief of them, and indeed the principal ornament of the town is St Paul's, which once had a college of prebendaries. There was a famous castle here, which was demolished in the reign of Henry VIII, and the site is now a bowling-green.

In *The Antiquities of England and Wales* (1798), Francis Grose remarked, 'the Ouse being made navigable enriches the town' and added, 'the south side has a market on Tuesday for cattle, and the north side one on Saturday for corn and other provisions'. Earlier in the 18th century, Daniel Defoe, in *A Tour Thro' the Whole Island of Great Britain* (1724), had observed, 'Here likewise is a great Corn-market,

2 An engraving of Bedford Bridge by Medland, from an original drawing by I. Walker, published in September 1794 by Harrison & Co. No. 18 Paternoster Row, London. A description of the bridge accompanied the engraving:

> The bridge, the only striking object in the town, is one hundred and sixteen yards long, and consists of seven arches: but it is so inconveniently narrow, that two carriages are unable to pass with safety; and so steep, that the drivers cannot see each other from the opposite ends.

and vast Quantities of Grain are brought here, and carried down by large Vessels and Barges to *Lynn*, where it is again shipped and carried by Sea to *Holland*.' Nathaniel Spencer, in *The Complete English Traveller* (1771), wrote, 'The trade carried on with Lynn by the navigation on the Ouse is very considerable', while *Pigot & Co.'s Commercial Directory* of 1830 referred to 'a tolerable trade in grain, coals and timber by river navigation, the Ouse being navigable for barges from hence to Lynn'. Around forty-five years later, *The National Gazetteer of Great Britain and Ireland* mentioned, 'A good trade is carried on with Lynn and other towns on the river, in corn and malt, coals and timber.' In 1895, the Ouse Transport Co., general carriers, were advertising their business conveying goods by water from Lynn to St Ives, Huntingdon, St Neots, Bedford and intermediate places. However, the Bedford Ouse had gone into decline. The owner could not obtain reasonable toll charges so he shut the locks and by 1900 trade on the river ceased.

Despite the closure of the locks downriver, Edwardian residents of Bedford made good use of their part of Great Ouse judging by old postcards of the town, which show a great variety of river scenes and activities. A century later, the Bedford River Festival is one of the events in the locality and, with the locks having been restored, Bedford is a destination for holiday cruisers and narrowboats. Here, two branches of the Great Ouse are linked by Bedford Lock and the river flows through an area of park and gardens, which is attractive to both locals and visitors.

An interesting account of boating down the Great Ouse appeared in P. Bonthron's *My holidays on inland waterways* (1916). The author chartered a 'roomy double-sculling skiff' for the trip from Messrs Cheetham and Biffen of Bedford as a motor boat could not be used on through journeys on the river due to poor conditions at the time. The start of the voyage was at 10.30am and there were 25 miles and 12 locks ahead to Huntingdon. Initially, the locks were managed without difficulty and the rowers found that the upper part of the river was attractive and that they could easily navigate it. However, trouble began some miles down due to weed in the river and it was so serious that on several occasions they lost trace of their course. These conditions continued downstream to Tempsford and shallows were also encountered.

The Great Ouse Catchment Board took over the navigation rights on the Bedford Ouse in the mid-1930s, with the aim of improving drainage to the land and the restoration of the locks. During the long restoration period, the river came under the jurisdiction of the Great Ouse River Board, then the Great Ouse River Authority and latterly the Anglian Water Authority. The restoration of Bedford Lock was carried out during 1955 and it was opened in 1956, while work started on Cardington Lock in 1962 leading to its being opened in 1963. Roxton Lock was opened by the Duke of Bedford in 1972 and 1976 saw the opening of new locks at Great Barford and Willington. When Castle Mill Lock at Goldington was opened in 1978 this completed the connection to Bedford.

C.F. Farrar resumed canoeing on the Great Ouse on 28 August 1920 and this time took two former pupils as crew, starting downriver from **Willington**. He recorded, in *Ouse's Silent Tide*, that, on this occasion, they found all the locks 'unworkable and much decayed' until St Ives was reached. After a portage over the Long Mills Lock, which some years back had been the only lock in use, they came to the long 15th-century stone bridge at **Great Barford** and saw the little inn overlooking the river, which would have been frequented by thirsty barge crews. Here the rush trade still appeared to flourish as the canoeists passed men mowing the rushes, while women sorted them into shocks of long and short rushes. It was at Great Barford that they found the worst portage as there was a deep drop below the lock and a barbed wire fence along the lock side.

Downstream of Great Barford Lock is Roxton Lock. The River Ivel, once navigable to **Shefford**, joins the waterway just below this lock. After this junction, the Great Ouse is crossed at **Tempsford** by two bridges carrying the A1 trunk road. One bridge was built of stone in the early 19th century and the other is a concrete structure, erected in modern times. In 1920, C.F. Farrar observed that 'innumerable motors' were passing across the bridge carrying the 'Old North Road', successors of the stagecoaches, which once passed this way daily. Nearby **Eaton Socon** benefited from the traffic on this road. At the height of travel by stagecoach, there were about twenty coaches passing through this village daily.

3   The three-arched 17th-century bridge at St Neots was said to have been built with stones from the Benedictine priory of St Neot. This old bridge no longer stands, having been replaced with a concrete bridge built in the mid-1960s. The *Half Moon Hotel* boathouse is on the left-hand side of this early 20th-century view. Later this hotel became the *Bridge Hotel*.

Eaton Socon's 19th-century mill was working until the early 1960s. After being disused for some time, it was utilised for boat building and later it was made into the *Rivermill Tavern*. After his canoe trip in 1920, C.F. Farrar wrote of a charming mill house and garden. He also mentioned the great earthworks, below the lock and the mill tail, where once stood a fortress as 'guardian of the river'. The author noted that, below the mill, the view opened up to show the stately church tower of **St Neots** and also the church tower of the neighbouring settlement, **Eynesbury**, remarking that the former tower rivalled that of Magdalen College, Oxford.

St Neots is situated on the east bank of the Great Ouse. The town takes its name from St Neot who died *c*.AD 875. When Leofric, the founder of the first priory in St Neots, wanted a relic to put in his new establishment, the saint's body was removed from Cornwall. This early priory was dedicated in AD 974. Later, members of the Norman de Clare family built a new priory on a site near the river and this was re-dedicated in 1113. When St Neots Priory surrendered in 1534, at the time of the Dissolution of the Monasteries, the 12 monks and the prior were given pensions. It is not known what happened to the remains of St Neot after the Dissolution.

In the 12th century, the monks of St Neots Priory had been granted the right to hold a weekly market where the town's market place is still located today. A timber bridge was built so that customers could cross from the other side of the river as well as to enable tolls to be collected from those coming to the town from the west. This was replaced by a timber and stone structure in the late 16th century, which was superseded by a stone bridge in the 17th century. A late 19th-century gazetteer described this bridge as 'a stone bridge of one central arch, with two smaller ones, over the stream, and continued by six other arches, forming a causeway over the marshy lands adjoining'. Today, a modern concrete bridge crosses the Great Ouse.

Pigot & Co.'s Commercial Directory of 1823 noted, 'The river Ouse is navigable from the port of Lynn to St Neots, and thence to Bedford. A considerable trade is carried on in corn, wine, coals, iron, timber &c.' This early 19th-century directory also recorded: 'The greater part of the town being only a few feet above the ordinary level of the river, inundations are sometimes consequent upon sudden thaws, or very heavy rains, to such an extent as to render a navigation of the streets not merely practicable but necessary.'

Today, craft using the river at St Neots include narrowboats and cruisers and there are facilities for boaters at River Mill Marina, Eaton Socon, St Neots Marina and Crosshall Marina, while boats are also kept at the Ouse Valley River Club. Trips on the river, aboard the electric cruiser, *Priory Belle*, are run at weekends and Bank Holidays during the summer months from Riverside Park at St Neots. At Riverside Park a walk, following the river downstream, can be taken along the Ouse Valley Way. This route first crosses St Neots Bridge, then takes in Islands Common and Lammas Meadow, which are sites of Special Scientific Interest, before recrossing the river at **Little Paxton** and making for Paxton Pits Nature Reserve. Here there are lakes, meadow and woodland alongside the Great Ouse, which support a variety of wildlife. The Ouse Valley Way is a long-distance path, from Syresham to King's Lynn.

Downstream of St Neots, near Little Paxton, C.F. Farrar and his fellow canoeists found a huge new paper mill, replacing the old wooden structure, which had burnt down not long ago. At the lock near the mill, they had to portage across the road and take care of vehicles coming around a blind corner. P. Bonthron found that, after St Neots, he and his crew had to haul their heavy skiff over a considerable distance at locks, which were closed. They were fortunate in that they came across a Cambridge boating party, travelling downstream, who were carrying three wooden rollers, each about a yard in length. The Cambridge boaters passed their boat over these rollers at the locks and kindly lent them to P. Bonthron and his party, which was a considerable help.

After Little Paxton, the Great Ouse passes **Great Paxton**, which is situated on a ridge on the east side of the river. Holy Trinity Church at Great Paxton was originally a Saxon minster and there is still work from that period in the interior of the building. Further downstream are the villages of **Offord D'Arcy** and **Offord Cluny**. The latter has Cluny incorporated in its name as Cluny Abbey, in Burgundy, owned the manor between the 11th and 15th centuries. C.F. Farrar observed 'a vast up-to-date modern brick mill' at Offord Cluny, which was flourishing, but, once again, there was portage for the canoes at the lock. Now, alongside the former mill, a lock with a guillotine gate has replaced the old Offord Lock.

The road leading west from the mill goes to **Buckden** where the Bishops of Lincoln once had a palace. The remains of this magnificent building include the outer and inner gatehouses and the Great Tower. Buckden gives its name to a large marina alongside the Great Ouse, which was completed in 1964. **Brampton**, the next settlement downriver, is on the same side as Buckden. Its claim to fame is its connection with Samuel Pepys, the 17th-century diarist, whose parents lived in Brampton and who was a pupil at the Free School in Huntingdon.

At Brampton, there is a lock and a former flour mill, now converted into a pub and restaurant. It was just past Brampton Mill that C.F. Farrar caught sight of the spires of Huntingdon across the Portholme Meadow, which stretches between Brampton, Godmanchester and Huntingdon. The 16th-century writer, William Camden, wrote of 'a meadow encompass'd with the *Ouse*, called *Portholme*, exceeding large (and a more glorious one the Sun never saw)'. Claims vary on the area of this vast meadow, one giving 365 acres and another 360 acres, while a third mentions 257 acres. Whichever figure is right, Portholme Meadow is said to be the largest lowland meadow in England. In the past, it was the venue for horse racing. Samuel Lewis, in

4   Bowyer & Priestly operated the steam mills at Offord Cluny and Buckden when this view was taken *c.*1910. The tall chimney has gone, but the Mill House and Mill Cottage remain, while the mill has been converted into residential apartments.

A Topographical Dictionary of England, noted: 'On this extensive plain, which forms one of the finest courses in the kingdom, races take place annually, commencing on the first Tuesday in August, and continuing three days.' Used during the First World War as an airfield, the meadow is now a Site of Special Scientific Interest as it is the habitat of a variety of wildflowers such as cowslip and snakes head fritillary. The best time to see them is in early summer before the long grass is cut for hay.

In early times, **Godmanchester**, situated by a ford, was the meeting place of three Roman roads, Ermine Street, from London to York, Via Devana to Cambridge and a military road from Sandy. A Roman fort was constructed and a settlement established. The ford was eventually replaced by a bridge linking Godmanchester with Huntingdon. In 1784 a causeway, leading to the bridge on the Godmanchester side of the river, was enlarged with two series each of eight arches, which allowed the passage of flood water. The six-arched bridge, built in 1332, was an important crossing place as it was on the main road between London and the north.

Writing about **Huntingdon**, Daniel Defoe observed, 'It is a great Thorough-fair on the Northern Road, and is full of very good Inns'. The centuries-old *George Inn*, with its wooden gallery and wide arch, was one of the renowned coaching inns, which served the Old Great North Road. *Pigot & Co.'s Commercial Directory* of 1823 noted that nine coaches left the *George* daily for destinations, which included London, Boston, Birmingham, Cambridge and Leicester. Although badly damaged in a fire of 1865 and having a 19th-century façade, the *George* retained some of its earlier features. Iris Wedgwood, in *Fenland Rivers*, commented that no coaching inn that she had seen had given her 'so clear a glimpse back into the splendour of the past and the vast stud required by those who could run four coaches daily to London'.

The delays on the river, encountered by P. Bonthron and his boating party, since they set out the first morning from Bedford, meant that they had to carry on travelling two hours after sunset. They reached Huntingdon, their destination, just as the town church clock struck ten and were glad to turn in at the *George Hotel* after an 'arduous day's work'. C.F. Farrar, however, cut short his canoeing trip in mid-afternoon in order to put up at the *Old Bridge Hotel*. He recommended this hostelry to anyone seeking a charming weekend retreat as one could laze, after lunch, in the delightful garden by the river. Afterwards, one could summon a boatman and go for a trip on the Ouse either east or west as both ways were inviting. The author noted that there were no signs of the once-busy water traffic from Lynn, but house-boats, sailing boats and punts were the order of the day.

The Great Ouse at Huntingdon is still a good place for pleasure boating and day boats, canoes and rowing boats are available for hire from several places on the river, while there are overnight moorings for visiting craft. Visitors to the town can take the Huntingdon Town Trail, a walk of approximately one and a half miles featuring places of interest such as the Cromwell Museum. Huntingdon is associated with Oliver Cromwell who was born in the town on 25 April 1599 and with the poet, William Cowper, who lived here with the Unwin family from 1765 until his

5   A peaceful scene on the Great Ouse at Huntingdon. Rowing boats and punts could be hired from Childs & Hall's boatyard on the Godmanchester side of the river.

move to Olney in 1768. It is said that **Hartford**, a short distance downstream of Huntingdon, was a favourite spot of the poet. Iris Wedgwood described Hartford as 'the cosiest place imaginable, with its thatched cottages and air of modest content', while C.F. Farrar thought that Hartford, with its horse ferry and the church tower in the background, was 'a peep into the land of Constable'.

The author of *Ouse's Silent Tide* was of the opinion that, although the Great Ouse, between Brampton Mill and St Ives, lacked the 'primitive solitude and charm' of the upper reaches of Tyringham, it nevertheless followed a beautiful course. P. Bonthron concurred that the country below Huntingdon right down to St Ives was as interesting as any that he and his fellow boaters had come across. However, they had four locks in their second day's run and over two of these they had to lift their boat, which was 'again a tedious operation'.

Riverside villages downstream of Huntingdon include **Houghton**, **Hemingford Abbots** and **Hemingford Grey**. Houghton is renowned for its water mill, which came into the possession of the National Trust in 1939. After being leased to the Youth Hostels Association for a number of years, it was opened to visitors. Wheat is ground here, during milling demonstrations, using power from the north waterwheel, the restoration of which took place in 1999. Houghton Lock, a modern lock with a guillotine gate, is situated near Houghton Mill, while the next lock downriver is Hemingford Lock. The latter was reconstructed on a new site and was the first to have an electric guillotine gate. Hemingford Mill was still standing in 1920 when C.F. Farrar described it as 'another ancient wooden relic of the past'.

Below Hemingford Grey, the author of *Ouse's Silent Tide* sighted **St Ives** and noted that one of the town's two church spires, that belonging to All Saints', had been shorn off after a low-flying aeroplane had crashed into it in 1917. Other accounts give the date of this aeroplane crash, in which the pilot died, as 1918. The spire of All Saints' parish church had suffered before, having been blown down in a gale in 1741. It was rebuilt in 1748 and again in 1879, while its reconstruction, after the crash, was completed in 1924. Most of the building of All Saints' Church dates from the 15th century, but there was a church here at the time of Domesday Book when the settlement was known by its ancient name of Slepe. A skeleton in a coffin, thought to belong to the seventh-century Persian Bishop Ivo, was discovered in the locality in around 1000 and a priory, named after the saint, was built at that spot. However, it was not until *c.*1200 that the name of the town changed to St Ives in commemoration of this saint.

There was originally a ford at St Ives, which was replaced by a wooden bridge said to have been built in the first decade of the 12th century. The present six-arched stone bridge dates from the 15th century and has a bridge chapel in the centre of it, one of only a few examples in the country. Other bridge chapels are at Wakefield and Rotherham. P. Bonthron, in *My Holidays on Inland Waterways*, remarked on the 'unique and striking character' of the bridges on the river, particularly those at St Neots, Huntingdon and St Ives, adding that the bridge at St Ives had a tower

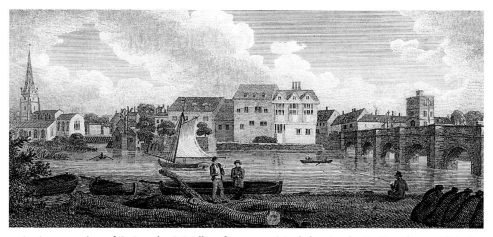

6   An engraving of St Ives, by I. Walker, from an original drawing by R. Harridan, published on 1 January 1802 by I. Walker No. 16 Rosomans Street, London. All Saints' Church is on the left and St Ives Bridge with its bridge chapel is on the right. In the foreground are river craft known as Fen lighters.

built on one of the parapets, which was occupied at that time as a residence. Since then the two extra storeys, which had been added to make a dwelling house, have been removed.

The Quay near the bridge, now used as a mooring by pleasure boats, was once used by trading vessels. In 1831, Samuel Lewis, in *A Topographical Dictionary of England*, stated that the trade of the town had become very considerable, especially in corn and coal. The author added, 'and, by means of the navigable river Ouse, an extensive commercial intercourse is carried on with Bedford, Lynn and other places.' In past times, commercial craft on the Great Ouse included Fen lighters. On average, these lighters were 42ft long by 10ft wide and could carry 25 tons of cargo. Fen lighters were linked together in 'gangs' of four or five behind a horse or in larger trains behind a tug. They were steered by one man who used a long steering pole attached to the second lighter, which extended over the stern of the leading lighter.

P. Bonthron, in 1916, mentioned that St Ives was 'the highest point up to which barges can now be navigated'. This was because of the decayed state of the locks. Writing about his trip in 1920, C.F. Farrar commented that the lock at St Ives was the 'first really workable lock', which he and his fellow canoeists had encountered since Bedford. He recalled an incident at this lock from his youth, 45 years earlier, when he was on a boating and camping trip to the Fens with friends. The St Ives lock keeper had lowered them down the lock and then demanded their lock pass. However, they had evaded paying for this at Bedford Lock since it cost 17 shillings to pass through all the locks to St Ives, which might have opened or might not have as the navigation on the Ouse was in decline. When the lock ticket was not produced, the lock keeper left the boys in the boat at the bottom of the lock for an hour or so in the hope that the money would be produced. Finally, as he couldn't keep them prisoner, the lock keeper compromised with the demand that they were to write to their mother or father explaining the position and that the 17 shillings should be sent by postal order to Mr Grey at St Ives Lock. The letter was never written and when, four days later, the boys returned to St Ives Lock they had to think up a ruse to get through without paying.

The lock keeper had noted that no postal order had been sent, but the boys pretended that C.F. Farrar, lying at the bottom of the boat, had been taken ill, having chalked his face to a 'ghastly pallor' and wrapped a wet towel bandage around his head. Saying that they could not carry on to Bedford and that the boat would have to be put on a cart and taken to the station, the lock keeper agreed to provide carriage for 10 shillings. Then when the upper lock gates opened and the boat cleared them, the pallid boy rose up and the conspirators sped away for dear life pursued along the bank by the lock keeper shouting and throwing stones and clods of earth!

The author of *Ouse's Silent Tide* thought that the seven miles between St Ives and Earith was a 'dreary stretch', now that navigation had almost ceased, with only the staunch at Brownshill relieving the monotony. His usual habit was to hire

7 Hermitage Lock, looking downstream along the Old West River, 2005. This lock between the tidal Great Ouse and the non-tidal Old West River is manned.

someone to ply his 'bark' between St Ives and Earith, while he went by train to meet it. There are, however, some interesting features to be seen before Earith is reached. **Holywell**, on the left bank of the Great Ouse, takes its name from the spring, which is near the church of St John the Baptist. Surrounded by a brick-built arched structure, erected in the mid-1840s, the spring is reputed to have healing powers. Holywell is also known for its ancient *Ferry Boat Inn*, which is said to be haunted by the ghost of Juliet Tewsley who hung herself, having been rejected in love by a local woodcutter in 1050. Tradition has it that her grave is beneath a large flat slab of stone on the floor of the inn.

The *Ferry Boat Inn* is named after the ferry, operated here in past times. A chain ferry or wooden drawbridge once carried foot passengers, animals and vehicles across the river. This was replaced by a smaller version in the 1930s, which was carried off in the raging floods of March 1947. The latter occurred after deep winter snow melted rapidly and this thaw, plus heavy rain, caused rivers to rise. Gales on the night of 16 and 17 March made the problems worse and, in the event, the river banks at Over were breached and thousands of acres of land were flooded. The breach was closed by the army a week later.

Not far downriver, at the *Pike and Eel Inn*, there was once a drawbridge-type ferry, too, called Overcote Ferry. Downstream of the site of this ferry, Brownshill Staunch, originally dating from 1834, is now a lock with two guillotine gates operated by electricity. It marks the beginning of the river's course across the low-lying Fens. Between this lock and Hermitage Lock, the Great Ouse is tidal. The river, from Bedford to Hermitage Lock, is often referred to as the Bedford Ouse, but after Hermitage Lock, the non-tidal waterway becomes the Old West River and, from Pope's Corner, it is known as the Ely Ouse.

Earith is on the tidal section of the Great Ouse. In the early years of the 20th century, this large village had a station at Earith Bridge on the Ely, Sutton and St Ives branch of the Great Eastern Railway. At this time, when the fen lands, adjoining the river, were flooded in winter, to the depth of a foot or more, they formed a famous skating ground when the water froze. Then, they were visited by thousands of people with special trains from Cambridge run for their use.

The distinctive low-lying area known as the Fens has a long and fascinating history. For centuries, the Fens were a swampy wilderness in which there were islands of higher ground where there were settlements. It was on such an island at Ely that the Saxon leader, Hereward the Wake, held out against the Normans. Legend has it that William the Conqueror crossed the marshes via Aldreth Causeway and that a battle was fought, between the Normans and the Saxons, near Aldreth High Bridge, which crosses the Old West River.

The agricultural Fens of today, which rely on drains, pumps and flood banks for flood control, are very different from the Cambridgeshire Fens about which the 16th-century writer, William Camden, made this comment:

> The upper and north-part of this Shire is all-over divided into river-isles (branch'd out by the many flowings of ditches, chanels and drains,) which all the summer-long afford a most delightful green prospect; but in winter are almost all under water, further every way than one can see, and in some sort resembling the sea, it self … The more southerly and the largest part of all that fenny Country which belongs to this Shire was called by the Saxons Elig, now the *Isle of Ely*, from the chief of these Islands. Bede derives it from *Eels* and some have call'd it the *Isle of Eels* … and others from *Helig*, a British word signifying Willows or Sallows, which it bears in abundance; and indeed they are the only thriving trees here.

Camden remarked that the willows were 'in great abundance, either growing wild, or set on the banks of rivers to prevent overflowing: which being frequently cut down rise again … with a very numerous offspring'. The pollarded willows were used for making baskets, while the Fens afforded 'great quantities of Turf and Sedge for firing, and Reeds for Thatching'. He wrote of the Fenmen as 'a sort of people (much like the place) of rugged inciviliz'd tempers … usually walking aloft on a sort of stilts' and all keeping to the business of 'grazing, fishing and fowling'. These traditional livelihoods were threatened when plans were made to drain the Fens in the 17th century to provide land for agriculture. At that time, groups of men known as Fen Tigers tried to disrupt the work of drainage.

During the draining of the Fens, the Dutch engineer, Cornelius Vermuyden, made two straight cuts from the Great Ouse at Earith. The first cut, known as the Old Bedford River, was dug to Salter's Lode. It was completed in 1637. At 21 miles long, it had a sluice at both ends. The New Bedford River or Hundred Foot Drain, the second cut, was dug parallel to the first channel in 1651 and a new sluice was constructed at Denver. These two cuts were named after Francis, the 4th Earl of Bedford who, with others, had appointed Vermuyden to drain the Fens. High barrier banks were built along the outer sides of the two cuts, making the great area between them a reservoir for flood waters. This area is known as the Ouse Washes and, as well as being important for flood control, is also noted as a wildfowl refuge. Today, there is no through navigation along the Old Bedford River, but the tidal New Bedford River is navigable to below Denver Sluice.

The draining of the Fens caused the rich black peat in the recently produced agricultural land to shrink so there were difficulties with natural drainage. Windpumps

8   The junction of the Cam and the Great Ouse, *c.*1880s.

were employed to lift water from the fields into the rivers. A surviving example of such a windpump is at Wicken Fen Nature Reserve, which is owned by the National Trust. Eventually, wind pumps were superseded by steam-driven pumps. A feature of interest near the village of **Stretham** is the former land drainage pumping station, now restored by the Stretham Engine Trust. The building houses a steam-powered beam engine, which was among over 100 such steam pumping engines used in the Fens to pump rainwater from the low-lying fields up into the rivers. Having been set up in 1831, Stretham Old Engine worked until 1925. It was used as a back-up engine until 1941 after which pumping was taken over by a diesel engine.

Stretham Old Engine is situated on the Old West River, which, from Hermitage Lock, follows a narrow and often winding course between high flood banks. At Pope's Corner, the Old West River meets the River Cam and the waterway becomes the Ely Ouse. At this junction, there is a riverside inn called the *Fish & Duck*. According to Michael Roulstone, in *Fenland Waterways* (1974), the history of this establishment dates back to the 13th century when monks from Ely used to frequent the ale house here.

Turning up the River Cam, the next hostelry is called *Five Miles from Anywhere, No Hurry*. This replaces the thatched public house of the same name, which once served river traffic and which burnt down in the 1950s. The unusual name of the public house is said to have become popular from *c.*1850. Originally the *Black Swan*, it was renamed after Lord Nelson during the first decade of the 19th century. Charles G. Harper, in *The Cambridge Ely and King's Lynn Road* (1902) described this public house at **Upware** as 'a queer building, partly ferry-house, partly inn'. There was once a chain ferry here, which the author referred to as an 'uncouth flat-bottomed craft'.

Boaters proceeding upstream pass channels called Lodes branching off from the east bank of the Cam. At Upware, a lock gives access to Reach Lode at the end of which is the village of **Reach**. Forking off from Reach Lode is Wicken Lode, which runs along the National Trust's Wicken Fen, and Burwell Lode leading to the village of **Burwell**. Both Reach Lode and Burwell Lode were once used for conveyance by water, especially for peat, which was used as fuel, and for clunch, a building stone. Further upstream are Swaffham Bulbeck Lode, navigable only as far as Slades Farm, and Bottisham Lode, leading to **Lode**, which is unnavigable. Both lodes were used for water transport in times past. Sedge for thatching was brought up Bottisham Lode, while corn was sent in lighters from **Swaffham Bulbeck** to King's Lynn.

Bottisham Lock is the first lock upstream on the River Cam. West of the lock is the village of **Waterbeach**, while upstream, on the opposite side of the river, is the smaller settlement of **Clayhithe**. The name of the latter suggests a landing place on the clay and, in past times, bricks were made at both Clayhithe and **Horningsea**, the next settlement upriver on the east bank. These bricks were loaded into lighters and transported by water. Centuries earlier, goods had been carried by water in this locality. South of Waterbeach is a short section of the Car Dyke,

9 May Races, *c.*1910. Douglas, the sender of this old postcard, wrote to Vera, 'I wonder if you can find me in this photo, it was taken at Cambridge May Races.'

constructed by the Romans and used as part of a waterway system connecting Cambridge with Lincoln.

The stretch of river between Baits Bite Lock and **Chesterton** is renowned for rowing races, which are watched by enthusiastic spectators some of whom take up their positions at the *Plough*, an attractive riverside public house at **Fen Ditton**. The races include the University races called the Lent and May Bumps, dating back to the 1820s, in which a large number of rowers participate over four days. The 'Lents' take place just before Easter, while the 'Mays' are held at the beginning of June. The boats line up with one-and-a-half boat lengths between them and the aim of each crew is to catch up with and bump the boat in front of them, while avoiding being bumped by the boat behind them. At the next day's race, the boats, successful in bumping, start before the boats, which were bumped. Over the four days' racing, boat crews can move up four places or more on the river. The finishing order of the race for any year is the starting order for the next year's race so the main aim is to keep a high position over the years with the hope of eventually becoming Head of the River.

In times past, **Cambridge** was not only famous for its University, but also for Stourbridge Fair, which was granted a charter by King John in 1211 and held annually on Stourbridge Common near the town. Daniel Defoe gave a lengthy description of this renowned fair in *A Tour Thro' the Whole of Great Britain*, noting that the shops were placed in rows like streets and that every sort of London retail trade was represented at the fair along with 'Coffee-houses, Taverns, and Eating-houses in great Numbers'. Wholesale dealers in woollen manufacture had booths or tents 'of a vast Extent', while a 'prodigious' quantity of hops was seen at the fair, which took up a large part of the field. The 18th-century author remarked:

> I must not omit here also to mention, that the river *Grant*, or *Cam*, which runs close by the North-west Side of the Fair in its way from the Fair-field, by Water carriage from *London* and other Parts; first to the port of *Lynn* and then in Barges up the *Ouse*, from the *Ouse* into the *Cam*, and so to the very Edge of the Fair.

Daniel Defoe further commented that great quantities of heavy goods, including hops, were sent from the fair to Lynn by water and from there shipped for the Humber, to Hull and York and for Newcastle-upon-Tyne and even to Scotland. However, by the late 18th century, Stourbridge Fair was not quite so important though its staple commodities such as wool, hops, leather, cheese and iron were still very considerable. In 1831, Samuel Lewis, in *A Topographical Dictionary of England*, added timber and cattle to this list of staple goods and noted that the fair continued for upwards of three weeks.

Cambridge, itself, was an inland port in bygone days with wharves near Magdalene Bridge and Silver Street Bridge. Samuel Lewis stated that at Cambridge a considerable trade in corn, coal, timber and iron was carried on with the port of Lynn, by means of the Cam. The author of *A Topographical Dictionary of England* also remarked: 'A great quantity of oil, pressed at the numerous mills in the Isle of Ely, from flax, hemp and coleseed, is brought up the river; and butter is also conveyed hither weekly from Norfolk and the Isle of Ely, and sent by wagons to London.' There was no towing path between Magdalene Bridge and Silver Street Bridge, as horses were not permitted in the college grounds on either side of the stretch of river called the Backs. Lighters had to be pulled along by horses walking through the river along a causeway under the water, which must have been an extraordinary sight.

The New and Complete English Traveller, published in 1794, gave a description of the bridges at the backs of the colleges in this University town:

> Cambridge, distant from London fifty-one miles, is situated on the banks of the River Cam, which divides it into two parts, that are joined by a bridge, and from whence it received its name. This bridge, which consists of only one arch, is built of stone and called the Great-Bridge, to distinguish it from another at the other end of the town, called the Small-Bridge. There is also a third, called Garret's Hostle-Bridge, which crosses the river between Trinity-Hall and the walks of that college. Besides these, there are six private bridges, which lead to the noble walks and gardens belonging to the colleges, four of which are of stone and two of wood.

The Great Bridge is now known as Magdalene Bridge, while Silver Street Bridge is the Small Bridge. Between the two bridges are St John's College New Bridge, familiarly known as the Bridge of Sighs, St John's College Old Bridge, also known as Kitchen Bridge, Trinity College Bridge, Garret Hostel Bridge, Clare College Bridge, King's College Bridge and Queens' College Mathematical Bridge. A leisurely trip along the Backs and under these bridges can be taken by punt, passing impressive college buildings, which are situated among lawns and gardens. It is said that this is one of the most superb stretches of river in the country.

Besides its college buildings, Cambridge has a number of other interesting features. The 12th-century Church of the Holy Sepulchre, known as the Round Church, is one of only four round churches, which exist in England. Another noteworthy church is Great St Mary's Church where students once received their degrees. The winding stairs of the tower can be climbed to obtain a fine view of some of the colleges and the market place. A variety of museums can be also be visited in Cambridge including the Fitzwilliam Museum, displaying Egyptian, Greek and Roman antiquities, the University Museum of Archaeology and Anthropology, the University Museum of Zoology, the Sedgwick Museum of Earth Sciences and the Whipple Museum of the History of Science. However, although the town attracts visitors to its architectural sights and educational establishments, to many people the draw of Cambridge is to the river, whether for punting or for rowing or as the destination of a trip by narrowboat or cruiser.

Upstream of Cambridge, the river is known as the Granta. Punts may be poled up to Byron's Pool at Grantchester, named after the poet, Lord Byron, who is said to have swum there. Grantchester is renowned for its link with another poet, Rupert Brooke, who spent time in the village. His poem, *The Old Vicarage, Grantchester*, written in 1912, ends with the memorable and often-quoted lines:

Stands the Church clock at ten to three?
And is there honey still for tea?

Back on the Ely Ouse, after the junction with the Cam at Pope's Corner, **Little Thetford** is passed on the west bank, while the unnavigable Soham Lode branches off from the east bank. Ely Cathedral, dominating the skyline, is a landmark seen for miles around the Fens. *The New and Complete English Traveller*, published in 1794, gave this description of **Ely**:

> The city is neither beautiful or populous, which may be owing, perhaps, to its situation; for though it stands on a rising ground, yet it is so near the fens and marshes, that the inhabitants are sometimes afflicted with agues ... The principal edifice in this city that attracts the notice of a traveller, is the cathedral, which, like most other Gothic structures of the like magnitude, has been built at different times.

Ely's original abbey was founded by St Etheldreda c.AD 673. She was a daughter of a king of the East Angles and the queen of Egfrid of Northumbria who had retired to the Isle of Ely to become a nun. This early abbey was sacked and destroyed by the Danes in AD 870 and it was not until a century later that Ely became a monastery for Benedictine monks. The building of the Cathedral was started in Norman times and continued over the following centuries, its great monastery flourishing until its dissolution in 1539. The monks at Ely were granted the privilege of holding a fair on St Etheldreda's Day and this included the three days before and after this day. Stalls were put up not only in the Market Place, but also in the streets and alongside the river, too. Traders converged on Ely for this renowned event. A feature of the Etheldreda Fair used to be the silken necklaces offered for sale called 'Etheldreda's Chains' or 'St Audrey's Chains'. The word 'tawdry' originates from the cheap showy finery sold at the fair.

Besides the Etheldreda Fair, the Market Place was, of course, used for Ely's weekly market. Edmund Carter, in *The history of the county of Cambridge, from the earliest account to the present time* (1753), recorded that the Saturday market 'is an exceedingly good one; it is well supplied with butcher's-meat of all kinds, butter, cheese, tame fowls, eggs, and with wild-fowl and fresh-water fish of all kinds in the greatest of perfection, at the cheapest rates.' This author remarked that the soil of Ely was very fruitful producing cherries, asparagus and potatoes and added:

> They grow besides great quantities of beans, peas, colliflowers, cabbages, arti-chokes, strawberries, &c. and they send prodigious quantities of onions yearly to *Sturbridge-Fair* ... For the convenience of carrying these and other heavy commodities, they have a fine navigable river called the *Ouse*, which joining with the *Cam*, runs by the east-side of the town down to *Lynn*: and into which many navigable rivers do discharge themselves ... so that from *Ely* they have water carriage to *Lynn, Downham, Stoke, Brandon* and *Thetford* in *Norfolk*; to *Mildenhal*, and St *Edmonds-Bury, in Suffolk*; to many parts of *Bedfordshire, Huntingdonshire* and *Lincolnshire* but especially to *Cambridge*.

Edmund Carter further noted that, for the convenience of passengers and heavy goods to and from Cambridge, there was a passage-boat. This went every Tuesday and Friday morning from Ely and set out on its return on Wednesday and Saturday at noon, the distance by water being about 20 miles and generally taking about six hours. Nearly a century later, *Pigot & Co.'s Commercial Directory* of 1839 stated that there was conveyance by water from Ely to Cambridge, Lynn, Northampton, Bury St Edmunds, Huntingdon and all intermediate places and that Crabb's Packet Boat left Ely every Tuesday and Thursday.

Ely was an important centre of river trade for many years. In *Fenland Barge Traffic* (1972), published by Robert Wilson, it was stated that a number of gangs of horse-drawn lighters were once based in Ely. This booklet noted that the Annesdale Wharf, alongside the *Cutter Inn*, was used for unloading cargoes like sand and gravel, while Waterside Quay, at a higher level, was used for cargoes, which did not need shovelling. There were also several private quays belonging to timber yards. After the railway came to Ely in 1845, a large dock was constructed near the station. This was accessed via a cut from the Great Ouse and could accommodate up to 300 barges. Falling trade brought about the partial filling in of this dock around the time of the First World War and more of the dock was filled in during the 1940s.

By the early 20th century, when navigation had declined on the Great Ouse, there was still some commercial traffic from Ely. *Kelly's Directory of Cambridgeshire* of 1916 noted that there was water conveyance by boats and lighters to Cambridge, Lynn, St Ives and Mildenhall. After the construction of the Queen Adelaide sugar beet factory, near Ely, in 1925, steel barges brought the sugar beet from the fields alongside the lodes right to the factory, while coal was brought by water from King's Lynn. According to *Fenland Barge Traffic*, water transport to the factory reached its height with around 150 barges and seven diesel tugs.

Pamela Blakeman, in *The Book of Ely* (1990), mentioned that boat building had taken place at Ely from the 18th century by the firms of Cuttriss, Ashberry, Eaves, Pond and Appleyard. Thomas Charles Appleyard, boat builder, was listed at Annesdale in *Kelly's Directory of Cambridgeshire* of 1916. In that year, P. Bonthron wrote, in *My holidays on inland waterways*, that he had been in conversation with a prominent boat owner in Ely, from whom he had learned that there had been more development with the motor boat at Ely than on any part of the river. Both boat owner and author agreed that there was every likelihood of pleasure boating increasing, here, as there were some very good stretches of water giving about 10ft of depth in some places. Today, Ely Marina with its many berths for pleasure craft shows that Ely is still a popular centre for boating.

Downstream of Ely, a different kind of boating takes place on a wide stretch of the Great Ouse, set between high flood banks, which is known as the Adelaide Course. This is where the Cambridge University boat-race crews train. On 26 February 1944, the Oxford and Cambridge University Boat Race was held here, rather than on the River Thames, because of the danger in London in wartime. The 1944 race was recontested by veteran crews from the Oxford and Cambridge Universities on

10   The sign outside Ely's *Cutter Inn* showed a ship when this early 20th-century view was taken. However, the name of the inn is thought to have been derived from the 'cutters', men who cut the new channel of the Great Ouse from Ely to Littleport between 1827 and 1830.

28 February 2004 and the event was watched by more than 4,000 spectators lining the river banks.

Work on the cut between Ely and Littleport, straightening out the river's winding route, began in 1827 and the new channel was opened in 1830. About half-way along the cut, on the east bank, is the Great Ouse's junction with the River Lark. In times past, this tributary was navigable as far as **Bury St Edmunds** and coal was one of the cargoes conveyed by water from King's Lynn. When cheaper coal was transported by railway, the navigation declined. Now the head of navigation is at **Jude's Ferry**.

Littleport, on the west bank of the Great Ouse, is the next settlement downriver of the confluence with the River Lark. The main claim to fame of Littleport is that this was where the Littleport Riots took place in 1816. In May of that year, men driven to despair by poverty and starvation rioted in both Littleport and Ely. Five of their leaders were hanged at Ely and a memorial to them on the church wall at St Mary's Church in Ely ensures that they are not forgotten. Littleport was also renowned as a centre of fen skating. Charles G. Harper, in *The Cambridge Ely and King's Lynn Road*, remarked that when the flooded fields were covered with a coating of ice it was possible to 'skate pretty well all the way to Lynn on the one hand and to Peterborough on the other'. In *Recollections of Littleport*, E.R. Gill noted that Mr Peacock, the founder of Hope Brothers' Factory, once skated from Littleport to Cambridge and back in a day. On the occasions when the surroundings formed a vast frozen lake, skating matches were held.

Charles G. Harper wrote of a 'single-span iron bridge of great width', which crossed the Great Ouse near Littleport. Having crossed the bridge, the author turned to the road on the left, which followed the river. He commented that the road was of 'the most peculiar kind' as it was below the river and protected from it by 'great grassy banks'. He observed that houses and cottages were few and far between and were built below the river banks. William A. Dutt, the author of *Highways and Byways in East Anglia* (1901), travelled the same road along the Great Ouse from **Southery** to Littleport. Before crossing the bridge to Littleport, he paused to examine some 'queer little houses' by the riverside. He saw that they were lopsided because of the subsidence of the land on which they were built. This gradual shrinkage of the land was a consequence of the drainage of the Fens.

In October 1976, the new Littleport Bridge, carrying the A10 road across the Great Ouse, was opened. Just under five miles downstream of this bridge, another tributary, the Little Ouse or Brandon Creek, enters the Great Ouse near the *Ship Inn*. This tributary was once navigable for 22½ miles as far as **Thetford** in Norfolk, but the present head of navigation is **Brandon** in Suffolk. In 1831, Samuel Lewis, in *A Topographical Dictionary of England*, noted that the navigation in its course to Lynn had been lately improved between Thetford and Brandon and that 'a brisk business is carried on in corn, coal, wool and other articles'. *The Post Office Directory of Cambridge, Norfolk & Suffolk* of 1869 stated that the river at Thetford was navigable for barges and that great quantities of coal and timber were imported through Lynn, while corn, malt and wool were exported. At this time, goods went by Murrell's barges to Lynn and thence to London by vessel. C.F. Farrar and his fellow canoeists turned up Brandon Creek and spent the night in the 'delightful riverside

11 Lighters on the Little Ouse, Thetford, *c.*1915. In the early 20th century, the Little Ouse at Thetford was navigable down to its confluence with the Great Ouse.

Swan Inn at Brandon' before paddling up the nine-mile stretch to Thetford. There they found a charming old-world town with its great mound, the Castle Hill, which, in the author's opinion, everyone must visit. The intrepid canoeists even managed to get some 15 miles further upriver than Thetford on that trip.

C.F. Farrar thought that the voyage along the Great Ouse from Littleport to Denver Sluice was deadly dull. This section of the river is known as the 'Ten Mile River' or 'Ten Mile Ouse' and its huge flood banks stand high above the low fenland with little to break the monotony. William A. Dutt, in *Highways and Byways in East Anglia*, mentioned that the river traffic was inconsiderable and that the only craft he had seen between Littleport and Southery were a couple of narrow barges, which were towed past by a 'decrepit little steam tug' and then moored near a farmstead where some wagons were waiting to unload. Concerning a bargee who came strolling along the river bank, the author wrote, 'He thinks the Ouse a 'dull' river, and that it flows through a dreary land.' The bargee preferred Lynn where there was a bit of life as he thought that country life was 'like living in a teapot and 'peakin' at the world through the spout!'.

Before Denver Sluice is reached, the River Wissey joins the Great Ouse on its east bank. This tributary, passing by **Hilgay**, is navigable to Stoke Ferry. In the 1860s, considerable business was done at the wharf in **Stoke Ferry** in corn, coals, malt and flour, but river trade declined later in the century. However, commercial traffic on the Wissey increased in 1925 when a sugar beet factory was opened at **Wissington**, which was served by tugs towing barges carrying coal and sugar beet. Nowadays, road transport is used by the factory.

The first barrier at **Denver Sluice** was originally constructed by Cornelius Vermuyden in 1651. It stopped the passage of tidal water up the Great Ouse, diverting it up the New Bedford River. Navigation was hindered and there was much criticism of the structure. The sluice was destroyed in 1713 when a considerable amount of flood water met spring tides at the barrier. Reconstruction of the sluice took place between 1748 and 1750 and again in 1832. Since then improvements have been made to this structure, which is important for flood protection and land drainage. Denver Lock is used by craft travelling to King's Lynn and by those boaters wishing to pass along the tidal water of the Great Ouse to nearby Salter's Lode Lock, which gives access to the Middle Level Navigations and the River Nene. A passage to Salter's Lode Lock can be made during a short time on either side of high water. In 2001, a new lock was opened at Denver giving access to the non-tidal Flood Relief Channel, which allows boat passage towards King's Lynn.

North of Denver Sluice, the tidal Great Ouse flows to King's Lynn, via **Downham Market**. In 1831, Samuel Lewis, in *A Topographical Dictionary of England*, described Downham Market as being 'pleasantly situated on the declivity of an eminence, about a mile to the eastward of the river Ouse, commanding an extensive view to the west of the fens, with which it is connected with an ancient wooden bridge'. A modern bridge now spans the river. The name of Downham Market suggests that it was once a centre for trade and the town was certainly long renowned, in past

12   The *Jenyns Arms*, on the left of this view of Denver Sluice, was formerly known as the *Ship*. George Brighton was its landlord when this photograph was taken *c*.1915.

times, for its large butter market. In spring and summer, great quantities of butter were sent up the river to Cambridge and from there to London, thus acquiring the name of Cambridge butter. This trade at Downham Market became obsolete when the butter market, held on Mondays, moved to Swaffham. During the 19th century, the Saturday market had greatly declined, too, due to the increase in the trade at the markets in King's Lynn, Dereham, Swaffham and Wisbech.

After the bridge near Downham Market, the Great Ouse is crossed by bridges at **Stowbridge**, **Wiggenhall St Mary Magdalen**, **Wiggenhall St Germans** and by two more bridges at King's Lynn. The headroom under these bridges varies with the tides so boaters cruising along this stretch of the waterway have to be aware of potential danger. C.F. Farrar had voyaged between Denver Sluice and King's Lynn many years previously and his memory of the trip was not pleasant. He recalled Magdalen Bridge and St Germans Bridge as being 'two ancient rickety wooden bridges', one of which was involved in a law suit when pedestrians fell through its rotting timbers and drowned. Although his son wanted to finish their voyage at King's Lynn, the author of *Ouse's Silent Tide* declined to pass their canoe through the lock at Denver Sluice.

P. Bonthron and his companions, however, sculled along the Great Ouse from Ely to King's Lynn on the third and final day of their trip and left early to catch the ebb tide at Denver Sluice. They just managed to do it after a hard piece of sculling. The author of *My Holidays on Inland Waterways* commented that the tidal way below Denver had deep uninteresting banks, which showed the great extent of the rise and fall of the tide. Coming down those last 14 miles he and his friends didn't meet a single craft of any sort. They reached their destination at King's Lynn at 5.15pm, having covered the 30½ miles, including stoppages, in eight and a half hours.

At **King's Lynn**, a modern road bridge takes the A47 over the Great Ouse. Downstream of this is the final bridge on the river. Connecting King's Lynn and West Lynn, the first bridge to be built here opened in June 1821 and was known as the Free Bridge or Cut Bridge. It crossed the Eau Brink Cut, a straight and deep channel, into which the Great Ouse had been diverted to avoid a considerable bend in the river. At over 800ft long, the Free Bridge was one of the longest wooden bridges in England. In July 1873, this was replaced by an iron bridge. Just over half a century later, the iron bridge was superseded by a reinforced concrete bridge consisting of three 120ft-long spans and two 70ft-long spans.

The confluence of the Great Ouse with the River Nar is downstream of this bridge. The Nar was made navigable in the second half of the 18th century and cargoes such as coal, timber, corn and malt were carried between King's Lynn and **Narborough**. In *The Canals of Eastern England* (1977), John Boyes and Ronald Russell noted that by the mid-19th century maltsters and coal and corn merchants, called Marriot, owned the navigation and had a wharf at Narborough. However, trade on this river decreased after the opening of the railway line from King's Lynn to Narborough in 1846 and the authors of *The Canals of Eastern England* stated that navigation to Narborough ended in 1884. Today, a walk can be taken along the Nar Valley Way, which stretches for 34 miles from King's Lynn to the Norfolk Rural Life Museum at Gressenhall.

13 The South Gate was one of the landward entrances into King's Lynn. In existence by the early 13th century, it was reconstructed in the 15th century and underwent further rebuilding later. This photograph of the South Gate was taken *c*.1906-10.

In past times, King's Lynn or Lynn Regis, the last town on the Great Ouse, was often called simply Lynn. The name of Lynn Regis distinguished it from three villages in its neighbourhood, **Old Lynn**, **West Lynn** and **North Lynn**. Before the reign of Henry VIII, it had been called Bishop's Lynn as it belonged to the bishop of Norwich. It obtained the name of Lynn Regis when it came into the hands of Henry VIII at the Dissolution of the Monasteries.

The Norfolk Tour (1786) by Richard Beatniffe gave the following description of the town:

> It is a large, rich, handsome and very thriving town, standing on the eastern bank of the Great Ouse, at about ten miles distance from the British Ocean. It is one mile and a quarter long from the South-gate to the Blockhouse, at Fisher's-end, and about half a mile from the river to the East-gate, which is the broadest part; it contains about 2,500 houses and 12,000 inhabitants, is encompassed on the land side by a deep ditch and an ancient wall; was formerly defended by nine bastions, and might now easily be made a place of considerable strength. It is divided by four small rivers, over which there are fifteen bridges. At the North-end there is a platform of twelve cannon, eighteen pounders, called St Anne's Fort, but there being no cover for the men, it could be of very little use, if the town was attacked from the river side.

The New and Complete British Traveller of 1794 was not so dismissive of the town's defences, noting:

> King's Lynn was considered a strong garrison before the modern art of fortification began to be practised, and there are still so many remains of the walls, that the place might be put in a position of defence in a few days. The harbour, however, is well guarded, and there is a battery, called St Ann's-Platform, at the North-end of the town, on which twelve great guns are mounted, which completely command the harbour's entrance.

Whatever the state of the defences, it appears that King's Lynn was a thriving port in the late 18th century. Its considerable trading links were described in *A New Display of the Beauties of England*:

> The situation of the fall of the Ouse into the sea, gives it an opportunity of extend-ing its trade into eight different counties, so that it supplies many considerable cities and towns with heavy goods, not only of our own produce, but imported from abroad. It deals more largely in coals and wine than any other town in England, except London, Bristol, and Newcastle. In return for these commodities, Lynn receives back for exportation a great part of the corn which the counties it supplies them with produce; and of this one article Lynn exports more than any other port in the kingdom, except Hull in Yorkshire. Its foreign trade is very considerable, especially to Holland, Norway, the Baltic, Spain and Portugal.

Charles G. Harper, in *The Cambridge Ely and King's Lynn Road*, noted the connection with Holland at King's Lynn, remarking that the port was 'full of queer gables and quaint architectural details brought over from the Low Countries'. The author referred to the beautiful Custom House, built by Henry Bell, as 'a work of art that in its Dutch-like character seems to have been brought bodily from some old Netherlands town and set down here by the quay'. Henry Bell, who was twice mayor of King's Lynn, was also involved in the construction of other buildings in the town. The Custom House, which is a reminder of the past importance of trade to King's Lynn, now houses the town's tourist office.

In the late 19th century, the chief exports of King's Lynn were corn, wool and sand for glass making, while the main imports were corn, coal, timber, deal, tallow, hemp and wine. Fish of all kinds, especially shell fish, were sent to London in large quantities. At this time, many of the inhabitants of King's Lynn were involved in fishing and in the coasting and foreign trade. However, manufacturing was carried on, too, the main industries being ship and boat building and rope and sail making. By the first decade of the 20th century, King's Lynn was still important in the corn, coal and timber trades. Then, exports were mainly corn, sand and coprolites to British ports and coals, machinery, implements and manufactured goods for the foreign trade. The principal imports included timber, maize, barley, linseed, cotton seed, oilcake and sugar. In 1907, the total value of all imports at King's Lynn was £1,241,876.

Today, cereals and timber are still handled at the Port of King's Lynn as well as a range of other cargoes. The port offers storage for cereals, pulses, animal feed and fertilisers, while timber and steel can be stored undercover in transit sheds. Alexandra Dock and Bentinck Dock can take ships up to a maximum length of 119m and 13.8m beam, with a draught of up to 5.5m and 3,500 dead weight tonnes, while Riverside Quay can take vessels up to 140m long with 20m beam, 5.5m draught and 5,500 dead weight tonnes.

The maritime history of King's Lynn can be explored in the town's visitor attractions, which include Lynn Museum, True's Yard Fishing Heritage Museum and the 17th-century Custom House overlooking Purfleet Quay. The port's links with the Baltic are commemorated in the 15th-century Hanseatic Steelyard, which was the warehouse of the Hanseatic League of Baltic Merchants. Its ecclesiastical history can be discovered in the ancient churches of St Margaret, All Saints and the Chapel of St Nicholas, while its architectural history is displayed in the Guildhall of the Holy Trinity, the Guildhall of St George, the merchants' houses and the Corn Exchange in the Tuesday Market Place.

Two miles north of King's Lynn, the Great Ouse flows into the sea at the Wash. It has travelled around one hundred and sixty-one miles from its source near Brackley, and about seventy-five miles from its limit of navigation at Kempston Mill, near Bedford. The river's journey, from source to sea, has taken it under old stone bridges and past riverside inns, centuries-old churches, former water mills and the once-bustling wharves of the settlements on its banks. Throughout its length the Great Ouse and its banks are steeped in history, but the marinas and locks used by the boaters of today, along with the flood control and drainage system of the area, make this a modern waterway, too, and it is fascinating to compare the present-day river with how it was in the past.

BUCKINGHAM

14   The ford and iron footbridge across the Great Ouse can be seen in this view of an old entrance into Buckingham, which dates from *c.*1915. The London Road Bridge, opened in 1805, took traffic away from this route resulting in a lack of trade for the nearby *Woolpack Inn*.

15   Dedicated to St Peter and St Paul, Buckingham's parish church is situated on Castle Hill, the site of an ancient castle. The church was completed in 1781, but some rebuilding took place in the 19th century when a chancel and buttresses were added.

16 This early 20th-century view looks down Buckingham's Market Square towards the Bull Ring and the Old Gaol. The shop of W.H. Smith & Son, stationers and newsagents, is to the left, while further down the slope, on the same side, is the *Victoria Hotel*. The 'Ironmongery Stores' are on the extreme right. A variety of horse-drawn and motor vehicles adds interest to the scene.

17 The Bull Ring was once the venue for sheep fairs, which were still held here into the mid-20th century. In this view, dating from *c.*1903, the shop of hairdresser Fred W. Swift can be seen. In past times, a saddlery occupied the premises behind the wooden fence, next to the hairdresser's.

18 Buckingham's castellated gaol was built in 1748 as Summer Assizes were held at the town. The assizes were held there for the next 100 years until they moved to Aylesbury, which became the county town. In 1839, the front of the gaol was extended to provide a residence for the superintendent. Now known as the Old Gaol, the premises house the town's museum and tourist centre.

19   The mill stream, *c*.1909. There were several boathouses along the mill race at Stony Stratford. The mill burnt down in 1985, but has been rebuilt as apartments.

20   This old postcard view of floods from Stony Stratford Bridge was sent from Stony Stratford on 2 July 1908. In the background, the building with a turret was at that time Fegan's Home for Orphaned Boys. The square tower of St Giles' Church can be seen on the right.

21 The tower of the church of St Giles is in the background of this view of Market Square, while a general ironmonger's shop has goods displayed on the pavement in front of the premises. The tree, known as Wesley's Tree, acquired its name as the 18th-century Methodist preacher, John Wesley, preached under its shade.

22 The Roman road, Watling Street, passes through Stony Stratford and was used by stagecoaches on the London to Chester and North Wales route. In bygone days, the town's High Street was busy and had a number of inns catering for travellers passing through the town. The *White Horse* can be seen on the left of this Edwardian view of High Street, while the inn signs for the *Bull* and the *Cock* are hanging outside these two hostelries further along the street. The phrase 'cock-and-bull story', meaning an unbelievable tale, is said to have originated in the town. This notion came from the days when stagecoaches stopped at the *Cock* and the *Bull* and travellers were heard rivalling each other by telling highly fanciful tales.

23 The history of the renowned *Cock Hotel* goes back centuries. It is said that a John Cok kept this inn during the late 15th century and that the name of the hostelry was derived from his name rather than from the bird on the sign hanging outside. Thomas C. Clarke was the proprietor of the hotel in 1907, but F.T. Clarke is the name on the sign in this old postcard view, which was posted in 1909.

24   In the late 19th and early 20th centuries, workers in Stony Stratford travelled the two miles to the railway works at Wolverton by steam tram. For a number of years the terminus at Stony Stratford was the *Cock Hotel*. This view shows a stationary steam tram engine with two trams on Wolverton Road.

WOLVERTON

25   In past times, Cosgrove Aqueduct, carrying the Grand Junction Canal over the Great Ouse, was known as the Iron Trunk. The aqueduct, a cast-iron trough, was built by the engineer, Benjamin Bevan, in 1809, to replace a masonry aqueduct, which had collapsed the previous year. The 101ft-long aqueduct still survives today and it is 15ft wide and 6ft 6in deep. This old postcard view dates from *c.*1915 and shows the entrance to a small tunnel under the canal.

NEWPORT PAGNELL

26 Newport Pagnell was on the route from London to Leicester and on the road between Cambridge and Oxford. In 1810, North Bridge, shown here, was constructed over the mill stream, while Middle Bridge was erected over a secondary channel of the Great Ouse. This occurred at a time when the coaching trade was important to the town. A toll-house was built between Middle Bridge and North Bridge so that travellers could pay tolls for the upkeep of the bridges.

27 Looking up High Street from North Bridge. On the right is the *Neptune Inn* with signs advertising 'Good Stabling & Loose Boxes' and 'A Pony & Trap To Let'. In the background is the 16th-century tower of the parish church, which is dedicated to St Peter and St Paul.

28 Tickford Bridge crosses the River Lovat a short distance before the latter's junction with the Great Ouse. Replacing a stone bridge, this iron bridge, constructed in 1810, was initially a toll bridge like North Bridge. In *Newport Pagnell: A Pictorial History* (1995), the authors noted that, after the bridge was built by Messrs Walker of Rotherham, its sections were first transported by ship to London, then taken by canal to Great Linford and from there by road to Newport Pagnell. This view dates from *c.*1916.

OLNEY

29   Olney Mill was a substantial stone building on five floors, while the mill house had three. The range of buildings belonging to the mill included an office, stables, wagon sheds and store rooms. There was also a cattle yard and cow shed at the rear of the premises.

30 The tall building on the right, alongside Olney's Market Place, was the home of the poet, William Cowper, between 1768 and 1786. Known as Orchard Side, it is now the Cowper and Newton Museum and houses artefacts concerning both William Cowper and the Reverend John Newton, a former slave trader. The latter, curate of Olney's parish church, was a long-time friend of the poet and they wrote hymns together as well as separately. Their *Olney Hymns* were published in 1779. The famous hymn, *Amazing Grace*, was written by Newton.

31 The Summerhouse was where William Cowper retreated to write his poetry and prose. The poet described it as being 'not much bigger than a Sedan chair'. The door of the Summerhouse opened on to a garden full of flowers such as pinks, roses and honeysuckles, while the window overlooked his neighbour's orchard. This engraving of the Summerhouse is from Thomas Dugdale's *Curiosities of Great Britain*, which was published c.1835.

TURVEY AND HARROLD

32 The border between the counties of Buckinghamshire and Bedfordshire is on Turvey Bridge. There has been a river crossing here since at least the 12th century, though the present stone bridge dates from the 17th century. The statue of Jonah, shown in this Edwardian view, was put in the river in 1844.

33 At Harrold Bridge, there are six arches over the Great Ouse, a short causeway and nine arches over the flood plain. The earliest reference to a bridge here is said to be in documents dating from the 12th century.

BEDFORD

34 The drawing for this illustration of Bedford Bridge was made in 1760, while the engraving was published by S. Hooper on 10 December 1783 and was used in *The Antiquities of England and Wales* by Francis Grose. Describing the bridge as it was in former times, the author wrote: 'It has seven arches, and near the centre were two gate-houses; that on the north being used for a prison, and that on the south served as a storehouse for the arms and ammunition of the troops quartered there.'

35 The north gatehouse on Bedford Bridge, as it was in 1761, is shown in this engraving, which was published on 1 May 1783 by S. Hooper and included in *The Antiquities of England and Wales*. Francis Grose noted, 'These gate-houses were taken down in the year 1765, and six lamps set up on posts at proper intervals.'

36 The first stone having been laid in 1811, the present Bedford Bridge was completed and opened for use by the public in 1813. It became free from toll in 1835. This view of the bridge dates from c.1923.

37 Pleasure steamers were often a feature of early 20th-century postcards of Bedford. The sender of this view, featuring the bridge and a steamer, was staying at London Road, Bedford. In his message, on the back of the postcard, he informed his bride-to-be that Bedford was a very nice place, but the lodgings were 15 shillings per week and it would be better if they married as it took a lot of money to be in lodgings!

38   Looking downstream, the Embankment, river and pleasure steamer, *Lodore*, make an interesting scene. This old postcard view, dating from *c*.1908, also shows the road along the Embankment leading to Newnham about a mile east of the town.

39   Embankment, river and pleasure steamer, *Alma*. The imposing twin-gabled building on the Embankment was the Town and Country Club, opened in 1885, which contained dining room, smoke, billiard, reading and writing rooms. The windows above the main entrance had a fine view over the river. In 1910, there were about 170 members.

40 Looking along High Street from Bedford Bridge, *c.*1914. When this photograph was taken, the premises of Thomas Barnard & Co., Bankers, were on the left at No. 2 High Street, while hairdresser, Antoine Stavinski, advertised 'Salons de Coiffure' on a sign outside his shop at No. 12 High Street. Murkett Bros., Motor Agents, were on the opposite side of the road at No. 3 and Norman Emerson, caterer and confectioner, was at No. 9.

41 In the 19th century, buildings in St Paul's Square, which were once occupied by the Grammar School, were purchased by the town's corporation and adapted for municipal purposes. The Town Hall is shown on the left of this early 20th-century view, while the entrance to St Paul's Church is on the right.

42 The exterior of St Paul's Church dates mainly from the 14th and 15th centuries, but the tower and spire were replaced in Victorian times. A noteworthy feature inside the church is a brass commemorating a benefactor to the town, Sir William Harpur, who died in 1573 and who was at one time a Lord Mayor of the City of London. Outside in the churchyard is the gravestone of Patience, wife of Shadrach Johnson, who died in 1717 at the age of 38, having borne her husband 24 children!

43 This Edwardian view of High Street shows Francis Gamman & Sons, House Furnishers at No. 85, Thomas Kenworthy Green, grocer at No. 87 and Hockney Brothers Drapers, at Nos. 89, 91 and 93.

44 The statue of John Bunyan, author of *The Pilgrim's Progress*, was erected on St Peter's Green and presented to the town by the Duke of Bedford on 10 June 1874. Designed by Sir J.E. Boehm, the statue was cast in bronze and stands on a square pedestal around which, on the front and two sides, are scenes from *The Pilgrim's Progress*.

45   Thousands of Highland troops arrived in the town on 16 August 1914 at the start of the First World War. This old postcard view shows them marching past John Bunyan's statue.

46   This souvenir postcard celebrates those who were doing their duty 'For King and Country' at Bedford. Unfortunately, many of these soldiers died in Bedford, rather than at the front, having succumbed to diseases such as measles, diphtheria, scarlet fever and pneumonia to which they had no immunity.

47   The Promenade, *c.*1910. A leisurely way of life is depicted here with rowing boats on the river and a lone cyclist passing the couple who are walking along the waterside with a perambulator and their dog.

48   In the early years of the 20th century, Bedfordians would take a walk along the 'Prom' dressed in their best clothes on Sundays and on high days and holidays. These five young lads look very smart in their straw boaters, as do the ladies in their wide-brimmed hats. The land between the road and the river was laid out with walks and ornamental flower beds and planted with trees, making a fine promenade.

49 Band Night on the river at Bedford, in Edwardian times, must have been quite an event, judging by the number of small boats surrounding the floating bandstand and the crowd of onlookers on the riverside.

50   River and Promenade, *c.*1914. Rowing has been enjoyed on the river at Bedford for many years. The Bedford Rowing Club, established in 1886, runs head of the river races and regattas here.

51   Great Flood, Embankment, 29 April 1908. The sender of this old postcard wrote: 'This is just a photo of the floods as they really were. A lady we know saw a big dining room table floating down the river.'

52   An iron suspension bridge for the use of pedestrians was opened in July 1888, linking the Embankment Gardens with Mill Meadows on the opposite side of the river. This old postcard view of the suspension bridge was taken *c.*1915.

53   When this early 20th-century postcard view was taken, smartly hatted ladies were paddling their punt near the second weir, while a pleasure steamer made its way upstream.

54 The weir, downriver of Bedford's suspension bridge, had two boat slides on the right so that small boats could be passed from one level of the river to the other.

GREAT BARFORD

55 This old postcard view shows the bridge at Great Barford. Seventeen arches carry the road from Bedford to St Neots over the Great Ouse. In the background is the church of All Saints.

EATON SOCON

56   The photographer of this early 20th-century lock view showed that one of the balance beams at Eaton Socon Lock was a handy place to take a rest. In the background, the roofs and chimneys of Eaton Mill can be seen. Today, Eaton Socon Lock is one of the 16 locks on the stretch of the Great Ouse from Bedford Lock to Hermitage Lock.

57   Eaton Mill, *c.*1906. This former flour mill is now occupied by the *Rivermill Tavern*, while a marina is located nearby.

ST NEOTS

58 In past times, there was trade on the river between Bedford and the port of King's Lynn. This old print of the Great Ouse near St Neots and Eynesbury shows a gang of boats being towed downriver. The parish church of St Neots is on the left and that of Eynesbury is on the right. Both of these churches are dedicated to St Mary.

59 This early 20th-century view of Brook Street shows the public wharf along Hen Brook with St Mary's Church in the background. On the extreme left is the *Bushel & Strike*, kept at this time by George Peacock. Further along is the *White Swan*, which in Edwardian times was run by Mrs Elizabeth Woodcock.

60 Rowing boats on Hen Brook, *c.*1917. Hen Brook is one of several tributaries entering the Great Ouse in the vicinity of St Neots.

61 Gill's Boathouse, at the confluence of Hen Brook with the Great Ouse, is shown in this riverside scene. The spot was known as House-Boat Corner. In 1910, Charles Gill, house-boat proprietor, was advertising 'boats for eight, six or four persons'. The house-boats could be hired by the week and this type of holiday was popular with visitors who came to St Neots by train.

62 This old postcard view of the Great Ouse looks upstream from St Neot's Bridge and dates from *c.*1912. Ivy, the sender, remarked: 'Don't you think this looks pretty? Florrie and I have spent our holiday on one of these house-boats.'

63   A lone rower makes his way towards the bridge past the houses at River Terrace, on the left. These were demolished in recent years and new homes have since been erected on the site.

64   In past times, the town of St Neots consisted mainly of three wide streets, several smaller ones and the large market square. The building with the bracketed clock, on the right of this view of High Street, was originally the Corn Exchange, which was built in 1863. Later it became the Pavilion Cinema.

65   For centuries, a Thursday market has been held in the spacious Market Square at St Neots. This view of the square dates from c.1912.

66   Market Square, *c.*1912. Looking towards the bridge, the *Half Moon Hotel* is in the middle distance. In 1910, George Frederick Stone was the proprietor here.

67 Bathing place, *c.*1906. In bygone days, men would often swim naked in the River Ouse at St Neots, which caused surprise and sometimes offence to visitors to the area.

68 The tall chimney of the paper mill, situated between St Neots and Little Paxton, is reflected in the river in this tranquil scene. In the early 19th century, two brothers Henry and Sealy Fourdrinier converted a corn mill here into a paper mill. They were the inventors of a new process in which paper could be made in a continuous roll rather than in single sheets. By the late 19th century, the paper mill was operated by the St Neots Paper Mill Company.

69   In 1912, the paper mill buildings were destroyed in a fire. They were replaced when a new paper mill was constructed.

GODMANCHESTER

70   Cruisers passing through Godmanchester Lock in August 2005. The first lock at Godmanchester was one of the locks on the river, which were built between 1618 and 1630 to make navigation easier past the mill weirs. The present modern lock has a guillotine gate at the upstream end of the lock.

71 This tranquil scene, looking downstream towards The Causeway and dating from *c.*1914, was taken from near Godmanchester Lock.

72 This view of The Causeway dates from *c.*1916. On the left is the Chinese Bridge, designed by the architect, Gallier, and originally constructed in 1827. The present bridge is a replica, which was built in 1960 by Godmanchester Borough Council. To the right of the bridge is the Town Hall, which was built in 1844 and enlarged in 1899. The spire of the parish church of St Mary the Virgin can be seen above the roofs of the houses on The Causeway.

73 The buildings on The Causeway were constructed over four centuries and have an interesting medley of styles. In the centre of this pre-1918 view is the *Royal Oak*, which was kept by Thomas Chapman in 1910.

74 Island Hall Chinese Bridge linked the 18th-century mansion, Island Hall, with its pleasure grounds. A replica bridge was built here in 1988. The old water mill can be seen beyond the bridge in this early 20th-century view.

75   This photograph of the old mill at Godmanchester was taken between 1910 and 1914. C.F. Farrar described the mill as 'another hoary timbered ruin' and the location as an 'enchanted backwater'. The mill was pulled down in 1927.

76   In 1910, Browns & Goodman operated the tall steam-driven flour mill at Godmanchester in the background of this view of Huntingdon Bridge. This mill no longer stands, but other mill buildings near the bridge have now been converted into apartments. House-boats can be seen on the river alongside the premises of Childs & Hall, boat builders.

HUNTINGDON

77   For centuries, the narrow medieval Huntingdon Bridge, joining Huntingdon and Godmanchester, was the only crossing over the Great Ouse. Carrying the Great North Road, the bridge must have been busy during times past. In this photograph, which dates from between 1910 and 1914, the six-arched bridge is the backdrop to activity taking place at the boatyard belonging to Childs & Hall.

78   Dating from *c.*1920s, this view of Huntingdon Bridge and High Street shows the *Old Bridge Hotel* on the left. In 1924, Charles Herbert Roberts was the proprietor of this hotel.

79   Huntingdon has two parish churches. St Mary's Church is situated in High Street between the bridge and All Saints' Church on Market Hill. Originally dating from Norman times, St Mary's Church was rebuilt in the 13th century. Its western tower collapsed in 1607, but it was not until 1620-1 that it was restored.

80   The tall spire of Trinity Church dominates this view of the High Street. On the left can be seen the sign for Pirkis & Son. In 1910, Pirkis & Son were listed in *Kelly's Directory of Huntingdonshire* as 'oil and color men, oil merchants and general hardware merchants & china & glass warehouse' with premises at 122 High Street. On the right is the sign for the *Crown Hotel* at 49 High Street. This hotel was kept by Charles Ernest Dale in 1910.

81 Trinity Church was also known as Trinity Union Chapel. It was built in 1868, at a cost of nearly £12,000, to serve both the Baptists and the Congregationalists. Constructed mainly in Ketton stone, with Bath stone dressings, its tower and spire reached a height of 181ft. This church no longer stands.

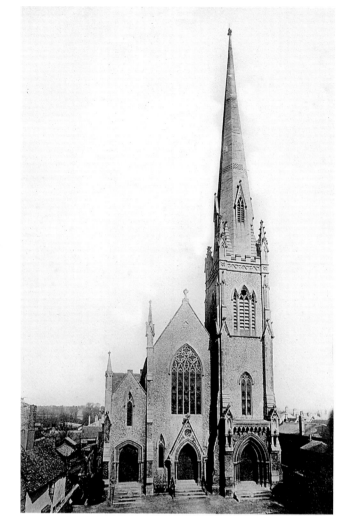

82 Market Hill and High Street, c.1922. Huntingdon's main street is its long High Street, which broadens at Market Hill. All Saints' Church can be seen in the background of this view, while the old Huntingdon Grammar School is across the road from the church, on the right.

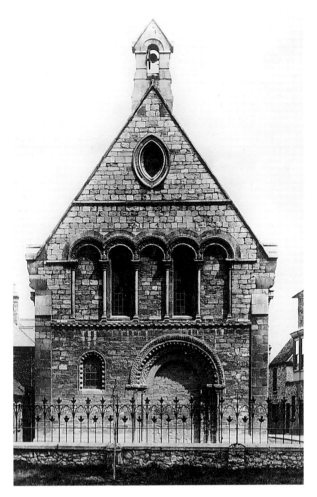

83 Grammar School, *c.*1916. Among the former pupils of Huntingdon Grammar School were Oliver Cromwell and the diarist, Samuel Pepys. The old Grammar School, shown here, was once part of St John's Hospital, which was founded by David, Earl of Huntingdon, during the reign of Henry II, to maintain and relieve poor people and to support a grammar school. Today, the Cromwell Museum is housed in this building.

84 The *George* was renowned as a coaching inn during the days of stagecoach travel, but had been in existence for many years before this time. Its cobbled courtyard, wooden gallery and open staircase made a charming scene on early 20th-century postcards. In 1910, Mrs Mary Jane Fisher was the proprietress of the *George*, which was advertised as a 'commercial & family hotel & posting house'. By 1924, George Henry Odell ran the premises and was 'caterer for luncheons, weddings, balls' besides providing 'motor cars on hire; loose boxes & lock-up coach house, garage, automobile clubhouse'.

85 Hartford Church, *c.*1916. The church of All Saints at Hartford is the setting for this peaceful riverside scene. Originally dating from Norman times, the medieval church has a Perpendicular tower. A chain ferry, which used to transport cattle across the river, was once situated just downstream of the church.

86   This evocative scene of rowing and fishing dates from *c.*1916. The fisherman was sitting on a bridge across Cook's Backwater.

87   Boating on the river, *c.*1916. The ladies were enjoying boating, while the gentlemen surveyed the river in this early 20th-century view, which arouses nostalgia for leisurely times past.

HOUGHTON

88 Houghton Mill, *c.*1905. A mill has stood on the site of Houghton Mill since late Saxon times. Reconstruction took place in the mid-17th century and there were a number of alterations made to the building since that time. The mill is associated with four generations of the Brown family who ran it from 1797 and during most of the following century. As well as giving employment at the mill to many local people, Potto Brown, who died in 1871, was instrumental in gaining a new school, a chapel and a water pump for the village of Houghton. The last miller, working at Houghton Mill, was Arthur Chopping who lived near the mill from 1915 to 1930. Houghton Mill is now owned by the National Trust.

89 In 1902, a shelter, topped by a turret containing a clock, was erected on the village green in memory of George W. Brown who had died in October 1901. The *George and Dragon* can be seen across the road from the thatched shelter. In 1910, this public house was run by Mrs Eliza Crain.

HEMINGFORD ABBOTS

90 The canoe was just about to be paddled under Black Bridge when this photograph was taken, *c*.1914. Adding interest to the scene were the two ladies and young girl, wearing wide-brimmed hats, who were standing on the wooden bridge.

91 St Margaret's Church, *c.*1914. Built in the Early English and Perpendicular styles, the western tower of the church at Hemingford Abbots is surmounted by a tall spire. The registers of the church date from 1693.

92 Hemingford Abbots is a picturesque village, which is well-known for its half-timbered and thatched buildings.

HEMINGFORD GREY

93   The approach by river to Hemingford Grey Church has, no doubt, been the subject of many photographs and paintings over the years. This old postcard view dates from *c*.1917.

94   Hemingford Grey's boat-house where, in 1910, Giddins & Son were boat builders.

95 The church at Hemingford Grey is dedicated to St James. Its tower was formerly topped by a spire, but this blew down on 8 September 1741 and only the base remains. The clock was put on the tower in 1884. Dating from c.1909, this photograph gives an idea of the peaceful location of the church.

96 The water mill at Hemingford Grey was said to have occupied the site of a former 12th-century mill, which was erected by the lord of the manor, Sir Reginald de Grey, after whom the parish was named to distinguish it from Hemingford Abbots. Hemingford Mill, which was situated near Hemingford Lock, no longer stands.

97 James Knights, miller and maltster, was living at Water Mill House, Hemingford Grey at the time of the 1871, 1881 and 1891 censuses. In 1871 and 1881, it was recorded on the censuses that he was the employer of nine men and two boys. In 1910, Thomas Knights & Son were millers here. This view of Hemingford Mill dates from c.1906-10.

ST IVES

98 Local children pose for the camera at The Waits against the background of All Saints' Church. Tradesmen with premises at The Waits in 1910 were Edward Anderton, butcher, Alfred Charles Bird, shopkeeper, James Brothers, plumber and painter, Arthur Hurl, beer retailer and carpenter, Albert Wallace Parfitt, shopkeeper and William Sykes, boot repairer.

99 Holt Island, on the opposite side of the river and to the left of this view, is just across the backwater from All Saints' Church. In past times, the island was an osier or willow bed, which gave work to a number of the inhabitants of St Ives. Men harvested the osiers and women stripped the willow. When the white willow was ready, it was transported to workshops to be made into baskets. Today, Holt Island is a nature reserve and a haven for a variety of plants, birds, insects and mammals.

100 The upstream side of the 15th-century six-arched stone bridge at St Ives is shown in this early 20th-century view. Two of the arches were reconstructed by William, Duke of Manchester in 1716.

101 The chapel on the downstream side of the medieval bridge had accommodation for a priest. Two extra storeys were added to the chapel during the 19th century to make a dwelling house, but these were removed during the following century. In 1910, the Manor House, the picturesque gabled and half-timbered building near the bridge, was the residence of Mrs Horatio Wadsworth. Across the road from the Manor House was the *Temperance Hotel*, run by the Misses Nellie and Hilda Wait.

102 There was a variety of trades in Bridge Street during Edwardian times. Occupations of people with premises there in 1910 included baker, butcher, cabinet maker, confectioner, dentist, fishmonger, pharmaceutical chemist, plumber, glazier and painter, provision merchant, tailor, watchmaker, jeweller and sight-testing optician. It appears that John Wadsworth of Bridge Street was a busy man as he was an 'aerated water manufacturer, cider merchant, ale & stout bottler & cordial manufacturer'. This view of Bridge Street dates from *c*.1908.

103   The buildings overlooking The Quay date mainly from the 18th century, a time when the wharf would have been busy with river craft. This early 20th-century photograph shows a quieter scene though the business of Water Carriers & Lightermen, St Ives Transport Co. Limited was at The Quay in 1910. At that time, the baker, James Judd Cotton, was also at The Quay. His premises were the second building from the left in this view.

104   The lighter, which was moored downstream of the bridge in this old postcard view, probably belonged to the Freear family of Stanground. At the time of the 1901 census, two members of this family, Christopher and James Freear, were recorded as barge owners, while Robert Freear was described as a retired barge owner.

105 The stone drinking fountain in the Broadway was erected by Elliot R. Odams of Fenstanton, Huntingdonshire, in memory of Queen Victoria's Diamond Jubilee in 1897. The fountain was presented to the town of St Ives on the coronation day of Edward VII on 9 August 1902.

106 In 1910, George Culverwell kept the *Robin Hood* public house, seen here on the left of this view of the Market Place, while on the opposite side of the thoroughfare, at The Pavement, Miss Mary Jane Rich was proprietress of the *Cross Keys* public house. The church with the tall spire is the Free Church, which was built 1864-5.

107 A bronze statue of Oliver Cromwell was erected, by public subscription, on the Market Hill. Commemorating 'A Townsman of St Ives 1631-1636', it was unveiled by Lord E. Fitzmaurice, MP, on 23 October 1901. The names of H.I. Hankin, mayor, and G.D. Day, Town Clerk, are also on the statue.

108 Cattle market, *c.*1918. St Ives was granted its market by royal charter in the late 13th century. In 1910, the town had a market every Monday for cattle, sheep and pigs. At this time, there were two annual fairs, on Whit Monday and on 11 October, during which great quantities of cattle, sheep and general goods were sold.

HOLYWELL AND OVERCOTE FERRY

109 The *Ferry Boat Inn* at Holywell, said to be one of the oldest inns in England, was built at a crossing place over the Great Ouse, which has been used for centuries. Legend has it that the Saxon leader, Hereward the Wake, crossed the river here during his conflict with the Normans. The premises used to comprise two separate dwellings with the inn looking towards the river and the ferry cottage facing westwards.

110 This photograph of Overcote Ferry shows a large vessel, which could transport horse-drawn vehicles. In the background is the 300-year-old inn, still in business and known today as the *Pike and Eel Inn*.

111   Overcote Ferry linked Needingworth, on one side of the river, with Over on the opposite side.

EARITH

112   The *Black Bull* can be seen on the left of this old postcard of High Street, which was posted in 1912. Joseph Robert Haddock kept this public house in 1910, while Thomas Harold James was landlord in 1914. In the latter year, Frederick Enderby was a grocer in High Street. The shop on the left of this view, with blinds over the windows, has F. Enderby above the doorway.

113　High Street, *c.*1907. The children in this old postcard street scene would have attended the public elementary school in the village, which had been erected in 1839. The master of the school in 1910 was Ernest Augustus Thomas, while the mistress was Miss Harriet Jackson. Average attendance at this time was 123 children.

RIVER CAM

114　There are three locks on the River Cam – Bottisham Lock, Baits Bite Lock and Jesus Lock. One of the balance beams of Bottisham Lock can just be seen in this photograph, which dates from *c.*1910. Near the lock was the *Green Man*. Thomas C. Stephenson kept this public house in 1916.

115 In past times, a ferry crossed the river at Clayhithe. A bridge was built here *c.*1872, which gave access to Waterbeach railway station. The inn at Clayhithe Bridge, near Waterbeach, became known as the *Clayhithe Bridge Inn*. In 1916, H. Parker was the proprietor.

116 Trim house-boats are moored to the river bank, above Baits Bite Lock, in this view of the river dating from the early years of the 20th century.

117 St Mary's Church stands near a bend in the river at Fen Ditton. Originally dating from the 14th century, the building was restored in the 1880s when the tower was taken down to its foundations and reconstructed. This river scene dates from *c.*1912.

118 Visitors to the May Races pose for the camera in their punts and on the river bank in this photograph dating from *c.*1914.

119 A pleasure boat was a good place from which to watch activity on the river. The onlookers were watching the May Races when this photograph was taken *c.*1914.

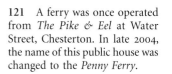

120 In the early years of the 20th century, the motor launch, *Enterprise I*, could be hired for private parties from H.C. Banham of 108 Regent Street, Cambridge.

121 A ferry was once operated from *The Pike & Eel* at Water Street, Chesterton. In late 2004, the name of this public house was changed to the *Penny Ferry*.

122 *The Pike & Eel* ferry at Chesterton was crowded with passengers when this photograph was taken in the 1920s.

RIVER CAM IN CAMBRIDGE

123 The college boathouses, which line the riverbank downstream of Victoria Bridge, can be seen from the towing path at Cambridge. In the middle distance of this early 20th-century view is Cambridge University Boat Club's Goldie Boathouse. This was named after J.H.D. Goldie of St John's who took part in four Boat Races against Oxford between 1869 and 1872.

124 The weir at Jesus Green divides the part of the River Cam, where punts and rowing boats are in use, from the stretch of the river, which is used by rowing eights and powered craft. The iron bridge across the river is for pedestrians.

125 This early 20th-century view of Jesus Lock shows the curved balance beams of the lock gates. Today, during the summer months, Jesus Lock is the limit of navigation for powered craft as the river above the lock is narrow and often crowded with punts.

126 Built in 1823, the cast-iron Magdalene Bridge stands at the site of the original river crossing after which Cambridge was named. The successive bridges at this crossing point were all known as the Great Bridge. This view of the bridge, Magdalene College and Magdalene Street dates from *c*.1905. Between the Great Bridge and the Small Bridge, further upstream, are the Backs. These are the back parts of the colleges, which extend to the Cam.

127 This print of New Bridge and St John's College appeared in *Le Keux's Memorials of Cambridge, A Series of Views of the Colleges, Halls and Public Buildings*, which was published in 1841. In the left foreground, a man poles a lighter towards the bridge, which is known as the Bridge of Sighs.

128 Old Bridge at St John's College was built by Robert Grumbold between 1709 and 1712. The Bridge of Sighs can just be seen beyond it in this pre-1918 old postcard view.

129 Trinity College Bridge was built in 1764, replacing a 17th-century stone bridge.

130 Garret Hostel Bridge, shown in this photograph, no longer stands. A new bridge with the same name was erected in 1960.

131 Clare College Bridge, designed by Thomas Grumbold, was erected between 1639 and 1640. It is the oldest bridge in Cambridge. This view of Clare College from Clare College Bridge dates from c.1908.

132 Ornamental balls along the top of the balustrades are interesting features on the mid-17th-century Clare College Bridge. However, one section of one of the large stone balls is missing. This old postcard of the bridge was posted in 1911.

133 This illustration of the River Cam and surroundings was engraved by W. and I. Walker from an original drawing by I. Walker and figures by Burney. It was published on 1 February 1793 by Harrison & Co. No. 18 Paternoster Row, London. The engraving shows laden Fen lighters being towed by horses wading along a causeway, which was constructed in the middle of the river. Clare College Bridge, Clare College and King's College Chapel are in the background.

134 The present King's College Bridge was built in 1819. Originally, there was a bridge at this location in the 15th century, but it was replaced several times.

135 The Mathematical Bridge at Queens' College is the only bridge made of wood on the Backs. Originally built in 1749, the second replica, shown here, was constructed in 1904. The building on the right is the President's Lodge, which dates from c.1460. This old postcard view was taken from Silver Street Bridge and posted in 1919.

136 This view of the river above Silver Street Bridge was taken *c*.1906-10. The cast-iron bridge was replaced by a modern bridge in the late 1950s. Silver Street Bridge is also known as Small Bridge. In this Edwardian view, there is a variety of small craft on the moorings of the *Anchor*, which had been both a public house and a place for boat hire since the latter half of the 19th century.

137 Punts, square-ended flat-bottomed craft, became popular on the River Cam during Edwardian times. While one person used a long pole to propel the punt, others could sit back and enjoy the scenery. F. Scudamore was among the forerunners of punt hire on the Cam, having established his business in the first decade of the 20th century. This photograph shows punting on Newnham Mill Pool, *c*.1914-18.

138 Grantchester Mill is said to have been built on the site of the mill made famous in *The Canterbury Tales* by Geoffrey Chaucer. A mill at 'Trompington, not fer from Cantebrigge' was mentioned in *The Reeve's Tale*. In 1916, miller James Nutter ran the mill at Grantchester and a lorry bearing his name can be seen on the extreme left of this photograph. When the water mill was destroyed by fire in 1928, large numbers of sightseers came to view the ruins.

139 Situated in a beautiful spot on the River Granta around two and a half miles west of Cambridge, Grantchester was a popular destination for boating picnics. Byron's Pool, especially, was a favourite venue.

140 This photograph of the sailing boat, *Freedom*, was taken near the bridge over the Great Ouse, which carried the Great Eastern railway line.

141 Ely Cathedral and the *Cutter Inn* from the river was a popular view on early 20th-century postcards. The small boats moored to the bank, in this view, show that the river at Ely was used for pleasure boating at this time.

142 Originally built on an island in the Fens, Ely Cathedral is a landmark, which can be seen for miles in the surrounding area. It is known as the 'Ship of the Fens'. This photograph of the cathedral was taken from the south-east and dates from between 1910 and 1914.

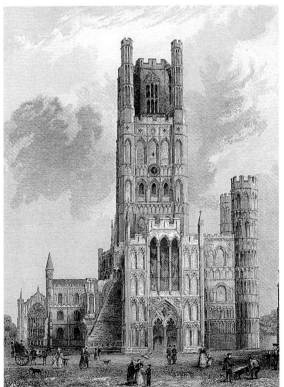

143 Ely Cathedral, West Front, drawn by R. Garland and engraved by B. Winkles for the part-work publication *Winkles's Architectural and Picturesque Illustrations of the Cathedral Churches of England and Wales*, which was published between 1835 and 1842.

144 In 1322, the Norman tower of Ely Cathedral collapsed. It was replaced by the stone Octagon, surmounted by the Lantern Tower, which was a masterpiece of carpentry.

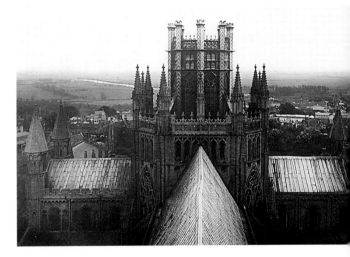

146 Ely Theological College was founded in 1876 and opened in 1881. The students at the college attended daily lectures given by the principal, vice-principal and chaplain, but there were no lectures on Saturdays or on saints' days. On Sundays, students read the lessons in Ely's churches and often preached at the district church at Adelaide Bridge. This photograph of the red-brick college building with stone facings dates from *c.*1912.

147 Dating from the 13th century, the half-timbered house, known as Oliver Cromwell's House, stands next to St Mary's Church. It was Oliver Cromwell's residence between 1636 and 1647. The house has been restored to show how the Cromwell family lived during this time. Visitors to the property can see eight rooms, which include the parlour, the kitchen, the study and the haunted bedroom. The building also houses Ely's tourist office.

148 In Edwardian times, the first shop on the left of this view of High Street was that of chemist, J.A. Gardiner, while shops further along the street, on the same side, included those selling shoes, drapery and ironmongery.

149 An early 20th-century view looking from the Market Place down Fore Hill to Waterside, near which was The Quay used by boats trading on the river.

150 This view of Broad Street shows half-timbered cottages with jetties and thatched roofs, which no longer stand. Next to them was the entrance to F.E. Chapman & Co., who were merchants dealing in English and foreign timber. The business had premises at Barton Square, Ely and at Bentinck Dock, King's Lynn, as well.

151   The *Cutter Inn* is a reminder of past times when it took three years for over 400 labourers to complete the task of cutting a new channel for the Great Ouse between Ely and Littleport. This Grade II listed building, in its attractive setting, is still a favourite venue on Ely's riverside today.

RIVER LARK

152   This early 20th-century postcard shows a Baptist Sunday School outing aboard a horse-drawn lighter at Prickwillow. According to writing on the back of the card, Bob Taylor was holding the horse and the minister was Mr Bilton.

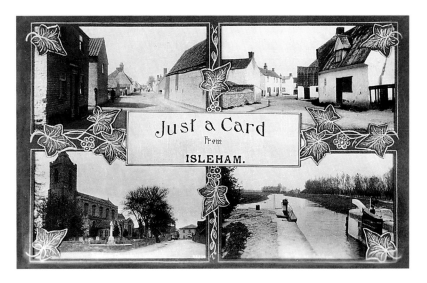

153 Dating from ancient times, the interesting village of Isleham is set back from the River Lark. Isleham Lock is shown on the right of this old multi-view postcard, while St Andrew's Church is on the left. The latter is renowned for its hammer-beam roof with 10 angels looking down and for its splendid memorial brasses.

LITTLEPORT

154 Main Street in the early 1890s had a number of tradespeople. Occupations then included beer retailer, boot and shoe maker, butcher, confectioner, draper, fancy draper, grocer, haberdasher, ironmonger, photographer and picture-frame maker, saddler and tailor. At this time, John Crabb kept the *Crown* shown on the left of this view of Main Street, which probably dates from a decade or so later.

155 On the right of this view of Granby Street is Littleport's Town Hall at the junction of Granby Street, Victoria Street and Main Street. The Town Hall was erected in 1879 by the Trustees of the Town Lands Charity. This building now houses Littleport Library.

RIVER LITTLE OUSE OR BRANDON CREEK

156 The Little Ouse joins the Great Ouse by the *Ship Inn*. Also known as Brandon Creek, this river, originally navigable to Thetford, was once controlled by eight navigation weirs. In the early years of the 20th century, George Graves was the landlord of the *Ship Inn* at Brandon Creek.

157 In ancient times, there was a ford over the Little Ouse at Brandon Bridge. The ferry, which replaced it, was superseded by a wooden bridge in medieval times, while a stone bridge was built here in the 17th century. This picturesque four-arched structure, shown here, was pulled down in 1953, along with the old maltings nearby, and the present bridge was opened in 1954.

158 This interesting river scene shows lighters on the Little Ouse at Thetford. In the background is the Town Bridge, while on the right is the Haling Path. In Edwardian times, the Little Ouse was navigable from Thetford to the Great Ouse.

159 Thetford's Town Bridge, which was once on the main road from London to Norwich, was built of cast iron in 1829, replacing an earlier wooden structure. Nowadays, the London road no longer runs through the centre of Thetford, but a reminder of the past can be seen in the former coaching inns in the town.

DENVER SLUICE

160 Iris Wedgwood, in *Fenland Rivers*, referred to Denver Sluice as an 'imposing object', noting that 'with its immense gates and heavy machinery it looks like a huge monster brooding over the waters it controls'. C.F. Farrar, in *Ouse's Silent Tide*, likened the massive barrier to some 'riverine Atlas' bearing up 'the ponderous weight of down-coming rivers'. This view of Denver Sluice dates from *c.*1915.

161 Designed by William Cunliffe of London, the clock tower was presented to the town by James Scott in 1878. The main and lower parts are octagonal, while the clock chamber is rectangular. Prominent in this Edwardian view is the shop of Herbert Wilson, the outfitter and clothier whose address was Market Square. Next to Wilson's is the *Swan*, in High Street, which was run by John Mason in 1908.

162 St Edmund's Church dates originally from Norman times, but has been extensively altered since then. The low battlemented tower is topped by a slender spire. When this early 20th-century photograph was taken, the tower and spire had been restored in recent years. This restoration took place in 1896 and cost £340.

KING'S LYNN

163 The first road bridge between King's Lynn and West Lynn was made of wood, while the second was made of iron. The latter was superseded in the mid-1920s by the 'New Bridge', shown here, which was made of concrete.

164 At the South Gate, the tall pointed archway was for horse-drawn traffic, while the two smaller openings were for pedestrians. The public house called the *Honest Lawyer*, to the right of the South Gate, was kept by Walter Dixon in 1908.

165 The hexagonal Greyfriars Tower in Tower Gardens is a remnant of the Franciscan friary, which was founded here in the 13th century.

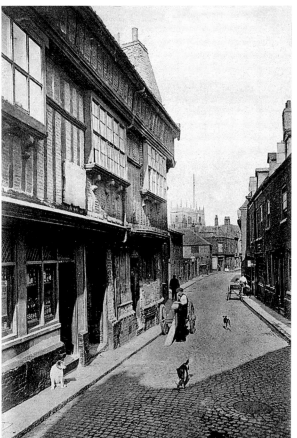

166 Legend has it that there was once a tunnel between Greyfriars Priory and the Red Mount, on the east side of the town, which is shown in this view dating from *c*.1904. This octagonal red-brick building has three storeys and houses two chapels. The chapel on the lower part is believed to have been erected in the 13th century, while the one on the top storey was built *c*.1484 and is known as the Chapel of Our Lady of the Mount. In past times, the Red Mount was much visited by pilgrims on their way to Walsingham.

167 This early 20th-century view of the narrow cobbled Bridge Street shows the *Greenland Fishery* public house, which was kept by Henry Rudd Crome in 1908.The timber-framed house was built in 1605 as a merchant's residence, but was later used as an inn. It derived its name from the period when it was frequented by mariners from ships, which sailed from King's Lynn into Arctic waters.

168 St Margaret's Church was formerly the church of a Benedictine priory, which was dedicated to St Mary Magdalene and St Margaret. Over the centuries, there has been much reconstruction of the church, especially after destruction caused by the fall of a spire from one of the western towers during the 18th century. Inside the building, features of interest include carved misericords and some fine 14th-century brasses.

169 This photograph of the Guildhall of the Holy Trinity, in the Saturday Market Place, was taken in the first decade of the 20th century. The Guildhall, its façade chequered in flint and stone, was erected in 1423, while the municipal buildings to the west of it were constructed during 1895-6.

170 The photographer was looking towards St Margaret's Church when he took this Edwardian view of High Street, in which motor traffic is noticeably absent. On the extreme right of the picture is the shop of Liptons Limited, provision dealers, while next door are the premises of Adcock & Son, tobacconists.

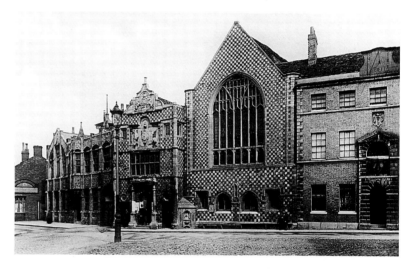

171 Built in 1683, originally as a Merchants' Exchange, the Custom House on Purfleet Quay used to be the headquarters of HM Customs and Excise at King's Lynn. This photograph of the freestone building, with its unusual roof topped by a small open turret, dates from *c*.1906-10. In 1907, the revenue collected here was £102,000.

172 In the early 20th century, cattle, corn and agricultural produce were brought to King's Lynn for shipment. During Edwardian times, when this photograph of the Tuesday Market Place was taken, there were two market days at King's Lynn, one on Tuesday and the other on Saturday. The Saturday market was held in the Saturday Market Place where produce for sale included meat, poultry and fish. Tuesday was the more important day as it was market day for corn and a livestock market was held in the cattle market near Broad Street.

173 William A. Dutt, in *Highways and Byways in East Anglia*, remarked that it was only from the west bank of the river that one could get a satisfactory view of Lynn and that the view was 'not without its elements of the picturesque'. A centuries-old warehouse at South Quay is on the right of this photograph, which was taken from the West Lynn side of the Great Ouse *c*.1909.

174 King's Lynn from West Lynn Harbour, *c.*1905. The author of *Highways and Byways in East Anglia* decided to cross the river to King's Lynn in one of the 'primitive ferry boats'. Today, more than a century later, a ferry still operates between West Lynn and King's Lynn.

175 In the early years of the 20th century, there were around 14 miles of sidings on Dock Company premises at King's Lynn and the overall acreage of the docks, quays and railways was more than 100 acres.

176 The Alexandra Dock, constructed between 1867 and 1869, was opened by the Prince of Wales on 7 July 1869. Located at the northern end of the town and adjacent to the harbour, it encompassed an area of about seven acres. A 250ft-long covered timber wharf was built on the south side of the dock. In 1908, around the time this photograph was taken, there were steam cranes at the wharf for loading and unloading cargoes, while at the end of the dock was a hydraulic lift used for the shipment of coal from the coalfields of Nottinghamshire and Derbyshire.

177 In 1881, work was started on an additional dock called the Bentinck Dock, which was opened in 1884. This new basin, measuring 1,000ft by 400ft, was linked to the old dock by a short canal and closed off by lock gates.

178 Fishing Fleet, c.1910-14. On 31 December 1906, there were 167 fishing boats registered as belonging to the port of King's Lynn and these boats gave employment to 383 men and boys. Fish caught at this time included sole, cod and smelt. Fishing boats still sail from King's Lynn today, but now the catch is mainly shellfish such as cockles, mussels and shrimps.

Bibliography

A New Display of the Beauties of England (1773)

Beatniffe, Richard, *The Norfolk Tour* (1786)

Blair, Andrew Hunter, *Great Ouse Country* (2002)

Blair, Andrew Hunter, *The River Great Ouse and tributaries* (2001)

Blakeman, Pamela, and Petty, Michael, *Ely* (1997)

Blakeman, Pamela, *The Book of Ely* (1990)

Bonthron, P., *My Holidays on Inland Waterways: 2000 miles cruising by motor boat and pleasure skiff on the canals and rivers of Great Britain* (1916)

Bowskill, Derek, *The Norfolk Broads and Fens* (1999)

Boyes, John and Russell, Ronald, *The Canals of Eastern England* (1977)

Camden, William, *Britannia: or a Chorographical Description of Great Britain and Ireland, Together with the Adjacent Islands.* (1586, Translation by Gibson, Edmund, 1722)

Carter, Edmund, *The history of the county of Cambridge, from the earliest account to the present time* (1753)

Carter, W.B., *The Restoration and Development of the Bedford Ouse* (2005)

Defoe Daniel, *A Tour Thro' the Whole Island of Great Britain* (1724)

Doig, Tom, *Huntingdon, St Neots and St Ives: Photographic Memories* (2004)

Dutt, William A., *Highways and Byways in East Anglia* (1901)

Edwards, L.A., *Inland Waterways of Great Britain* (6th edn 1985)

Farrar, C.F., *Ouse's Silent Tide* (1921)

Gill, E.R., *Recollections of Littleport* (nd)

Grose, Francis, *The Antiquities of England and Wales* (1798)

Harper, Charles G., *The Cambridge Ely and King's Lynn Road* (1902)

Hunt, Julian, *Buckingham: A Pictorial History* (1994)

Kelly's Directory of Bedfordshire (1910, 1914)

Kelly's Directory of Cambridgeshire (1912, 1916)

Kelly's Directory of Huntingdonshire (1910)

Kelly's Directory of Norfolk (1908, 1912)

Kitchener, Lewis, *The Heart and Soul of Olney* (2004)

Lewis, Samuel, *A Topographical Dictionary of England* (1831)

Luxford, Nita, *A Working Life on the Great Ouse* (2000)

McKnight, Hugh, *The Shell Book of Inland Waterways* (2nd edn 1981)

Manning, S.A., *Portrait of Cambridgeshire* (1978)

Meeres, Frank, *Ely & The Fens: Photographic Memories* (2003)

Mynard, Dennis and Hunt, Julian, *Newport Pagnell: A Pictorial History* (1995)

Nicholson/The Ordnance Survey Guide to the Broads and Fens (1986)

Pigot & Co.'s Commercial Directory (1823, 1830, 1839)

Roulstone, Alan and Roulstone, Michael, *Fenland Waterways* (1974)

Rouse, Michael, *Edwardian Ely* (1981)

Scarfe, Norman, *Cambridgeshire: A Shell Guide* (1983)

Simper, Robert, *Rivers to the Fens: Rivers Cam, Great Ouse, Nene and other Waterways* (nd)

Spencer, Nathaniel, *The Complete English Traveller* (1771)

Summers, Dorothy, *The Great Ouse: The History of a River Navigation* (1973)

The New and Complete English Traveller (1794)

The Post Office Directory of Cambridge, Norfolk & Suffolk (1869)

The Universal British Directory of Trade, Commerce and Manufacture (1791)

Ward Lock and Co., *A New Pictorial and Descriptive Guide to Cambridge and District* (nd)

Wedgwood, Iris, *Fenland Rivers* (1936)

Wilson, Robert, *Fenland Barge Traffic* (1972)

Young, Rosa, *St Neots Past* (1996)

Index

View of the City of Ely in the County of Cambridge. Engraved for *The Modern Universal British Traveller* (1779).